IMPACT

INSIGHTS, EFFECTS AND THE REALITY OF IMPAIRED DRIVING

RESPONSIBLY DRIVEN DUI PROJECT

IMPACT: Insights, Effects and the Reality of Impaired Driving

Copyright © 2018 Responsibly Driven DUI Project

All rights reserved. No part of this book may be reproduced in any written, electronic, recording, or photocopying form without written permission from the publisher.

ISBN: 978-0-9997662-0-0

10 9 8 7 6 5 4 3 2 1

Printed in the United States of America

Library of Congress Control Number: 2018905908

Other than the first names of each inmate and those individuals who have contributed their perspective, most of the names in the book have been changed in an effort to protect the privacy, and to ensure the safety of the individuals included in these testimonials. With the appropriate permission, some full names are included.

Responsibly Driven DUI Project Coordinator:
Christopher Martinez
Edited by: Jonathan P.M. Barber
Marketing Coordinator: Juan Covarrubias
Cover Design by: RAM Photo/Graphics, Tucson, AZ
Interior Layout by: 322 Creative

Fiesta Publishing | fiestapublishing.com

Dedication

To Vanessa, Arlo, Catherine, Carla, Gyla Jean, their families, and all other people who are unnecessarily killed and harmed by impaired drivers.

TABLE OF CONTENTS

Foreword 1
Introduction 4
Juan 9
Eduardo 13
Allie 17
Cari 22
DeVyon 27
Gerardo 28
Mark 30
Peter B. 33
Jennifer.. 39
Sergio 42
Brian 48
Darrell 54
Charles... 59
Leroy 64
Conrado 67
Rae Ellen 71
Kellie 74
Jonathan G. 79
Raymond 82
Deborah... 85
Chris R. 91
Eric 95
Law Enforcement Officer 98
Heather... 101
Douglas... 107

Chris M.	110
Edward	117
David L.	119
Michael	123
David T.	126
Nancy	133
Jim	137
Peter W.	139
Jonathan B.	144
Mother of a Fatal DUI Hit and Run Driver	149
Paul	153
Daniel	157
Maria	163
Rudy	168
Stephen	171
Hernan	176
About the *Responsibly Driven* DUI Project	179
Letter from the Publisher	180
Acknowledgements	182
Appendices	185
Acronyms and Terms	187
Discussion Questions	191

FOREWORD
Impaired driving is a leading cause of death in the United States of America.

Every fifteen minutes another person dies or is injured in an auto collision caused by an impaired driver. In a blink of an eye, families are torn apart and lives forever impacted due to an individual's irresponsible decision to drive impaired. Besides the unmeasurable human loss and suffering, the tragic aspect of impaired driving is that it is one hundred-percent preventable. In response to this crisis, numerous driving under the influence (DUI) prevention campaigns have spawned and a series of punitive measures have been enacted across the nation. Why have these attempts barely stymied the growing trend of impaired driving? Why has the public not heeded the dire lessons of impaired driving's impact?

In 2014, I was part of a group of DUI murderers, at the Correctional Training Facility (CTF), located in Soledad, California, who came together in an attempt to answer these exact questions. Let me be honest, our initial intention was self-serving. We were seeking these answers to better prepare for our upcoming parole hearings; however, as our conversations progressed, our intention shifted. We found that, as a group, we really wanted to find a solution to the impaired driving problem. We believe the answers can be found in a thorough analysis of impaired driving's two fundamental components: 1) the decision to become impaired and 2) the decision to drive impaired.

Denial makes it difficult to uncover the rationale behind these two decisions. It is the biggest obstacle inhibiting accountability because denial provides us, the impaired driver, comfort. Denial perpetuates a false sense of security. We would rather protect our inflated ego and maintain our chaotic lifestyle than acknowledge the severe consequences of our decisions and address our underlying issues. The truth of the matter, we refused to admit that we were dangerous drivers who callously put the lives of others and our lives at risk. Because of this truth, we spent a lot of time practicing empathy for our victims in our group meetings.

The breakthrough came when we discovered the real intentions underlying our choices to drink alcohol and/or use drugs and then drive impaired. We found that we constantly chose to attend to our immediate desires; we intentionally chose convenience and comfort over personal and public safety. Although this realization is shameful and deplorable, it reveals an opportunity to better ourselves. If we intentionally choose to become intoxicated and then to drive impaired, then we possess the power to choose something else. For us DUI murderers, that something else is a clean, sober, safe, and sustainable lifestyle, which centers on the enhancement of the lives of others. This begins with a commitment to make amends to our victims, our family, our community, and ourselves.

Why have previous DUI prevention campaigns not worked? They have not identified or addressed the core issues behind impaired driving – the impaired driver's distorted thinking and his/her detachment from the grave consequences of impaired driving. Much of that distorted thinking is predicated on self-absorption and an irrational sense of invincibility. The common thought, "It will never happen to me," grants the impaired driver permission to get behind the wheel while another common thought, "I'm not hurting anyone," creates a huge disconnect between the act of impaired driving and its potential to harm.

The following collection of testimonials from DUI offenders is an attempt to resolve these two core issues: distorted thinking and a detachment from its consequences. Some of the testimonials reveal the impaired driver's faulty logic and selfish value system. The hope is that by reading about the authors' experiences, thoughts, and feelings, other impaired drivers, or potential impaired drivers, will discover their faulty beliefs and become responsible before it is too late. Also, we hope any remaining semblance of denial will be dispelled by the testimonials from people affected by impaired driving. Impaired driving is not a victimless crime. It impacts the very fabric of society and our sense of safety.

The intent of this book is to bridge DUI offenders with readers in hopes of establishing a greater awareness and creating a dialogue for effective DUI prevention. Let's turn the existing negative consequences of impaired driving into a positive impact.

Jonathan P.M. Barber, CADC-CAS

INTRODUCTION

Recently I was asked, "Why did you decide to compile a book of impaired driving testimonies?" In that moment, thoughts and words escaped me. The actual preparation for this book started two years ago, and many of those weeks honestly, flashed by like a lightning bolt. My schedule of rehabilitative programs such as vocational classes, self-help groups, parole board preparation, and Church activities kept me quite busy. Even now, as I reflect over the book's development process, I am left pleasantly astounded. This book has been in the making since the day I murdered an innocent woman while driving under the influence (DUI) of alcohol.

Since then, many people have invested much time and effort into my positive transformation, and that is where the answer ultimately lies. My positive transformation occurred in four stages: a complete surrender to Jesus Christ as my Lord and Savior; working the Twelve-Steps of Alcoholics Anonymous (A.A.) seriously for the first time in my life; participating in the *Responsibly Driven* self-help group; and finally, attending The Urban Ministry Institute's (TUMI) Bible College. So here is my story:

I turned my life over to God soon after the fatal auto collision. I couldn't live with the feelings of guilt, shame, and despair that plagued my every thought. I did not know what to do or who to turn to for help. In my darkest hour, I completely surrendered not only my life, but also my will to Jesus Christ. Some people may scoff at jailhouse religion, but a radical change occurred within me overnight. Being extremely grateful for His grace, I wanted to share this gift of mercy with others. Eventually, I became a chapel clerk, a full-time leadership role at the Donovan State Prison. I was learning to live my life for God's purposes, not for my old selfish hedonistic desires.

The closer I grew toward Jesus, the more I realized that I possessed several unresolved internal issues, mainly, my history of substance abuse and impaired driving. In the past, I attended court-ordered A.A. meetings and DUI schools, but I refused to admit that I was an alcoholic or an addict. I worked hard, drank hard and played hard just like my chosen peers. They were not alcoholics or drug addicts. They were tough, hardworking construction men (or so I told myself). Moreover, DUI tickets were just an expensive, pain in the rear traffic ticket. Although, I was going through the motions to fulfill my court orders, I still didn't think the laws applied to me or that I had a substance abuse problem. The reality was, my chosen peers had multiple DUIs, but they had not murdered anyone. I murdered someone because I had been living in denial.

Now as a murderer, I needed to figure out where and why my life went wrong. What had happened? I was broken, so I surrendered to my Higher Power and began to genuinely work A.A.'s Twelve-Steps. The Twelve-Steps program is transformative in the sense it compelled me to face my underlying issues, which I had formerly swept under the rug. My journey of self-discovery drew me closer to the Lord and shed light on my self-deceptions.

A.A.'s Twelve-Steps advise alcoholics to integrate all its spiritual principals into other areas of one's life besides addiction. For me, that meant looking into my destructive behavior of impaired driving. Fortunately, I was transferred to the Correctional Central Training Facility (CTF) in Soledad, California, where the program, *Responsibly Driven,* is specifically designed for and offered to impaired drivers. The facilitators in this self-help program supported me by understanding that responsibility and amends could be attained through the identification and modification of my various mental narratives.

This was a paradigm shift for me. During one particular group session, we engaged in a brainstorm exercise where the facilitators listed on a whiteboard the myriad of mental narratives that we used in order to justify our decisions to drive impaired:

"I'm a good driver, even when drinking."

"It's no big deal. I'm only a little buzzed. I'm okay to drive."

"I'm only driving a short distance. I'll be home before anybody knows I'm impaired."

"I won't hurt anyone."

As the facilitators continued to scribe more statements, I swore the group was reading my mind. I had said all of those statements to myself. Hearing and seeing my thoughts on the whiteboard was truly a sobering and humbling experience.

Week after week, I began to acknowledge the strength of my denial. Before, while attending DUI schools, I refused to accept that I was a danger to society and myself. Being stubborn and prideful, I knew my thinking was not faulty and that I was not an alcoholic/addict. I was a good citizen. I worked and paid my bills. I wasn't a criminal! The *Responsibly Driven* exercises and group discussions shattered my façade. Ironically, a class taught by DUI murderers, helped me realize I was a self-centered, hedonistic man. I was only concerned with my needs and desires, regardless of the consequences of my actions. With this revelation, I realized I could never make up for the precious life I had taken, but I could help others. I knew that other impaired drivers needed the lessons of *Responsibly Driven* and to *hear* the men's testimonials of responsible transformation.

Around the same time that I started participating in *Responsibly Driven* I enrolled in TUMI's Bible College. I needed to stay immersed in my Biblical studies, in order to keep my commitment to Christianity (God) and sobriety. These commitments have helped me reconcile what I had done. They were the beginning of me making amends.

Besides developing my knowledge of the Gospel, TUMI presented a wonderful opportunity when an instructor assigned a project based upon the question, "What can you use from your past to positively affect society today?" Immediately, I knew the subject of my project. My past is full of substance abuse and twenty years of DUI activity that culminated in the tragic death of an innocent woman, the mother of four children. The good cause would be the prevention of impaired driving. In order to accomplish this goal, I was going to disseminate impaired driving testimonials to DUI schools, rehabilitation centers, and any other place people may be prone to DUI behavior.

I initially collected two testimonials from *Responsibly Driven* members, Jim Crawford and Gerardo Palacios. We sent our testimonials to over two thousand DUI Schools and rehabilitation centers. The response was amazing! Numerous instructors explained how the testimonials infused intrigue and enthusiasm into their classrooms. Several students wrote back expressing gratitude for the impactful stories and even had questions for us. We gladly replied through their instructors explaining why we had continued to drive under the influence, even after attending the same classes in which they were now involved. What really surprised me was the multiple requests for a book full of impaired driving testimonials. In particular, Edward Collins, a DUI counselor from Lucky Deuce DUI School, encouraged me to pursue this venture. He saw the project's potential before I did.

I was not going to miss the message on the wall. I sent out hundreds of flyers to all of California's prisons requesting testimonials from DUI offenders. To facilitate the collection, my sister, AMB, along with my old high school teacher D. Po. (whom I used to drink with, but is now sober himself) and his wife, S., started a publishing company called Amends Publishing.

The testimonials were temporarily posted on Amends Publishing's website. In order to obtain other publishers' perspectives and feasibility, I sent inquiries to one hundred and fifty publishers and exchanged an array of ideas about the book's marketability. The idea that made the most sense was the addition of testimonials from other individuals affected by impaired driving. Impaired driving is such a tragic crime and causes so much devastation, a book without these individuals' voices would be deficient and incredulous. I am so humbled and grateful that so many people joined in this effort to help prevent senseless future deaths by DUI crime.

Back to the original question, "Why did you decide to compile a book of impaired driving stories?"

Throughout my incarceration, I incrementally discovered the answer. My Christian faith has helped me understand the power of empathy, remorse, and reconciliation. My practice of A.A.'s Twelve-Steps has mitigated my character defects and repaired my relationships. My participation in *Responsibly Driven* has exposed my denial and erroneous thinking and has assisted me in creating new mental narratives for my life. My involvement in TUMI's Bible College has prompted me to transform my words into actions.

With these lessons in mind, the simple answer to the above question is that I want to **SAVE LIVES!** I destroyed a family in 2004, and the anguish that I have caused them resides deep in my heart. I do not want any family to feel such sorrow and pain. My hope is that the reader gains insight into the motivation and faulty thinking of the impaired driver and develops a real understanding of impaired driving's destruction.

The voices contained in this book paint a clear picture. *Hear* the authors' words, feel their emotions, and see their visions. Impaired driving is not a natural occurrence; therefore, we possess the ability to prevent it. Unfortunately, with the legalization of marijuana and the current prescription drug epidemic, impaired driving rates are on the rise. I truly hope this book begins a fruitful discussion on how best to combat impaired driving. Innocent lives are at stake!

Christopher Martinez

IN HIS OWN WORDS

My name is Juan and my mother raised me in California. At the age of fourteen I joined a party crew. Known for throwing epic parties in the county and despite our reputation of hosting wild keggers, I avoided alcohol. Back then, I was the one friend who didn't drink. Even though I attended parties, I was the designated driver for my friends because I was scared and thought if I drank, I would become like my father. He was an alcoholic who physically and mentally abused my mother.

I graduated high school in 2000 and a year later I started working at an auto insurance company that afforded me the luxury of traveling. During a vacation in Mexico when I was twenty years old, I started to drink alcohol. I thought I was old enough to handle my drinking. I thought since I worked hard that I was entitled to drink and party. After all, I wasn't harming anyone.

I started partying with my friends and became less responsible. Also, I started drinking and driving. At first, I got away with this crime multiple times. I recall leaving a local baseball stadium after a game, a ten-minute drive from my home. I blacked out and woke up entering the Mexican border with no recollection of the last two hours. Most people would have realized they were driving drunk and stopped to call for help, a taxi, or a friend to drive them home. I now realize that a responsible person would have recognized they had a drinking problem and would have started attending Alcoholics Anonymous (A.A.) meetings or checked themselves into a rehabilitation center.

Instead, I drank and partied for two days straight. I refused to believe that I had an alcohol problem. After all, I had never been in any legal trouble. I thought I had my life under control and was a law-abiding citizen. Soon after my binge partying began, my legal problems started. In 2007, at twenty-six years old, I got my first driving under the influence (DUI) ticket. I was upset as I knew I'd have to pay fines of up to four thousand dollars and be ordered to complete DUI school. I was angry. At the time, I thought it was just an easy way for the court system to make money. I didn't think I was an alcoholic and continued to drink and drive, because my partying was more important to me than a DUI ticket (I now realize this is a selfish and stupid way of thinking.).

My drinking increased as the years went by. I was partying five times a week, yet I still wouldn't admit I was an alcoholic. In 2009, I was celebrating my twenty-eighth birthday with friends and when I left the restaurant, was pulled over. I instantly thought, "Crap, not another DUI!"

I was arrested and charged with my second DUI. For the first time, I came face to face with the possibility of going to jail or prison. The thought of months behind bars scared me, so I bailed out. All I could think about was how and what I could do to avoid doing jail time. I hired a lawyer. He suggested that I get an ankle bracelet that would monitor my alcohol consumption. But it was a useless attempt on my part, because I wanted to manipulate the court system into believing I was making an effort to stop my alcohol use. I was hoping the judge would be lenient towards me. This didn't work. I was sentenced to three months of house arrest. I ended up spending fifteen thousand two hundred dollars on my second DUI.

How much money do you make in a week? How many weeks would you have to work to pay for a second DUI ticket? After all this, I was still in denial and not willing to accept that I was an alcoholic. I knew I had a drinking problem, but an alcoholic to me was hobo, a *low-life,* and someone without a job.

My friends and I thought drinking was a normal way of life. I took pride in being a *party animal* and *weekend warrior.* You would have thought that after spending large sums of money, I'd wake up and rethink my whole life. I should have checked into a rehabilitation program. Instead, I refused to acknowledge my ugly truth. I selfishly continued to party and drink. I had two DUI arrests and been arrested numerous times – two drunk in public arrests, a vandalism arrest, and a trespassing arrest, which were all alcohol related.

I now realize I was in denial all those years. I told myself that DUI tickets were just bad luck. I also thought I was too good of a driver to hurt anyone, so I didn't have to stop driving drunk. I figured I'd just pay the fines and keep better watch for the cops next time.

So, what will you choose? Will you remain in denial and possibly kill another person and/or yourself, or will you learn from my story?

In 2010, I was pulled over after leaving a club. This time there was no avoiding incarceration and I was sentenced to nine months in county jail. I was released in 2011. I lost everything. I had no job, car, or place to live. I moved in with my mom until I got back on my feet. For the first time in my adult life, I was sober and genuinely trying to do good. Have you ever come to a point in life where you want to do good, but it just seems bad things keep happening?

I didn't want to get into any more trouble with the law, but I refused to stop drinking with my friends. I was stuck in a rut and didn't know how to get out. My good intentions only lasted a few months. In 2012, I was at a club and it was time to leave, but I wasn't ready to go home. I wanted to party all night. My friends from the club got a cab and wanted me to leave with them, but I was stubborn and headed to a house party in another county.

After being there until the early hours of the morning I decided to leave. My cousin tried to stop me as he attempted to take my keys, but I left anyway. I'm ashamed and embarrassed to admit that I was so *hammered,* that I can't remember anything that happened next. I drove in a blacked-out condition and rear ended a vehicle, which caused the gas tank to explode. The whole car was engulfed in flames. The owner was trapped inside and burned to death. I'll never forget what the detective told me, "I don't know

Arizona Department of Transportation

if you believe in God, but you better start praying, for you murdered a woman."

I will forever be haunted by the fact that she endured a horrific, painful, tragic death that was due to my selfish, uncaring ways. I cringe every time I think of the life-threatening danger the whole community experienced because I only cared about my partying and ignored the obvious warning signs. The woman I struck that night was a daughter, sister, aunt, and a friend. She deserved better than to be murdered by an irresponsible alcoholic.

I cannot begin to fathom the pain and loss I have forced onto her family. I robbed her of a lifetime of happiness with her loved ones and all the memories they would have created together. I deeply regret that they will now have to endure a lifetime of pain, sorrow, and grief because of my cowardly act. I am profoundly ashamed of how I hurt her family and for the lasting pain I have caused each of them. I am the source of their heartbreak. It is because of my self-centered behavior that her family never got to say goodbye to her.

I chose to ignore all the warnings signs of drinking and driving which ultimately resulted in the death of an innocent woman. I am justly serving a life sentence, not knowing if I'll ever go home. I deserve to be in prison because I kept driving drunk after four DUI tickets. Ask yourself, "Am I selfishly ignoring the potential deadly consequences of my actions?"

I heard a saying that deeply impacted my life, "A smart man learns from his own mistakes, but a genius learns from other people's mistakes." Any of you who have a first or second DUI or have an alcoholic history, I'm pleading with you; be a genius and learn from my mistakes. Stop drinking and driving so you won't kill an innocent person and end up in this concrete and barbed-wire cocoon known as prison.

IN HIS OWN WORDS
Eduardo

To those of you who have driven impaired, seen a friend drive drunk, taken a court-ordered DUI class, or if you just like to party and have a good time, trust me, you'll want to read my story.

My name is Eduardo, and I'm a convicted murderer for killing an innocent woman whose whole life was ahead of her. This didn't just happen out of the blue, it wasn't an accident. It was a choice I decided to make that was irresponsible and selfish. Not only did I destroy her life and her future, but I also destroyed the lives of her family, friends, and every single person that knew her. I callously murdered her existence and stole the relationships she had with her loved ones who knew the joy and happiness of her company.

As you're reading this story, you may be saying to yourself, "Oh, that can never happen to me." Well, that's what I used to think. Do yourself a favor, don't drink alcohol and drive. Open your heart and mind. Read and *hear* what I'm writing. You could end up in prison too. Save a life, save your own, and heed my warning. Prison is a miserable and deplorable place. You don't want to end up here.

> **NEVER SAY 'THAT WON'T HAPPEN TO ME'. LIFE HAS A FUNNY WAY OF PROVING US WRONG.**

Don't be a jerk by being irresponsible like me. Make the right decision to have a designated driver before you start drinking or using. There are other ways to get home: call a friend, a taxi or Uber. There are options that don't involve getting behind the wheel of a car and driving. Once you start drinking alcohol, you impair your ability to think responsibly. You can easily end up like me in eight-foot by twelve-foot concrete tomb.

I grew up in a loving family of five. When my mom divorced my father, he was not really in my life. I remember watching my dad drink alcohol, get mad, and hit my mom and us kids. It confused and scared me. I wanted my dad to love me and to do the *father and son* things with me. Sadly, his drinking was more important. I learned to hate my dad's drinking.

As for my teenage years, I didn't really pay attention or know anything about drugs and alcohol. I started hanging out with my so-called friends and began drinking at the age of sixteen. For the next thirteen years, I loved to party, hanging out with friends and chasing girls. My whole life had become a party scene.

Forgotten were the days of my dad's alcoholism and what it caused. I didn't realize I was following in his shoes. I enjoyed getting *tore up,* drinking until I passed out. My friends and I thought it was *macho* to party every weekend. I was a party animal. I worked in order to buy and drink alcohol. My whole purpose in life was about the party.

Then I met my girlfriend. We enjoyed smoking weed, getting drunk, and just having a good time. My problem was that I didn't want to stop drinking. My goal every weekend was to get wasted until I passed out. My girl never left my side. I knew she was embarrassed for me when I acted like a fool. Deep down, I hated that she saw me *wasted* all the time, but I didn't know how to stop. I didn't want to stop. I told myself, "She either loves me the way I am, or she could *kick rocks.*"

There were times when she would try to pull me away from my friends because they always encouraged me to *party hard.* Sometimes we ended up in a fight. The day I realized that I was in love with her, I stopped hanging out with my friends as much and started spending more time with her. She had put up with a lot of my crap; yet, she still treated me good. But, I wasn't willing to stop my drinking. Now it was just her and I partying together at clubs, dances, and restaurants. I was happy and content, never thinking I had a drinking problem.

All that took a turn when she was diagnosed with brain cancer. Her diagnosis didn't matter to me, I loved my girl! She was my best friend and I vowed to stand by her side, taking her to her doctor's appointments and watching her suffer through the radiation and chemo treatments. The treatments weren't working, and it was tough on her. We always hoped for the best, but always received bad news. It broke our hearts. Deep down I knew I was losing my best friend, little by little and day by day.

As hard as I tried, this affected our relationship. I became depressed and drank my sorrows away. I knew I should have been strong for her, but I didn't know how to deal with the situation. Alcohol was my only solution. I told myself I was just easing the pain of watching her go through everything. What hurts me the most, she never complained.

One night, I got into an argument with her. I knew she was going through a lot and I should have been supportive. My anger toward the whole situation got the best of me. I decided she was better off without me. I thought it would be better to leave her and go to my mom's house, which was only a ten minute drive away. I told her to call me if she needed anything. I had been drinking, so by this time I was drunk and not in my right mind. (Take note: as soon as you take the first couple of drinks or smoke a joint, you are not in your right mind, you're impaired.).

I took off. I thought I was doing the right thing. Wrong! As I drove, I blacked out. I ran a red light and drove into the passenger side of a car. For the next three days, the person I collided with clung to life, but in the end, she died from my careless, drunken, self-centered behavior.

My heart sank when I was told she had died. I couldn't believe I had killed someone's daughter, sister, aunt, and cousin. She could have been your relative who I killed with my impaired driving. Think about that for a moment. The fact that I killed a person tore me apart, because I never thought I was a bad person or a criminal. Growing up, I thought I was just one of the guys, doing guy things. Partying wasn't evil. All I wanted was to have a good time, be fun loving. I never wanted to hurt anyone. But, that doesn't change the fact that I was irresponsible and careless. There is no reason to ever drive while impaired.

Yes, my girl was dying, and I didn't know how to deal with it, but that doesn't give me the right to place other people at risk. Any time someone, even if slightly buzzed, gets behind the wheel of car we put the whole world at risk. Since I was unable to face this truth, I was a murderer just waiting to kill someone because I drove drunk all the time. The sad part is that I didn't really care. I only thought about what I wanted and how I was feeling. Most of the time I used alcohol to escape from my reality. I could have very easily asked my mom, step-dad, or even my brother to pick me up.

When someone is drunk or high, responsible thoughts go right out the window and they become a menace to society. Every day, there are thousands of people driving buzzed or drunk, not thinking about its consequences. Most of the time they just don't *give a rip,* I didn't. All I cared about was my selfish needs, wants, and desires. I'm so ashamed of my attitude. I look back and realize this shocking truth. This is why I'm compelled to write my story and share my experiences. This could happen to anybody! If you can see yourself in my story in anyway, then wake up and *listen* to what I am writing. My pride and egotistical selfishness took an innocent life. I can never bring her back. I have to live with my choice to drive drunk and its consequence of pain, anguish, death and prison for the rest of my life.

I sit in prison writing this testimonial, hoping and praying that it will reach just one person. If you recognize anything from my story and can relate it to your own life, get help! It's not a crime to ask for help. Go to an A.A. meeting and discover how to deal with life's problems sober. You are not a weak person to get a sponsor. Seek help and learn how to a live new life; one that does not put people in jeopardy every day. If you have even a slight drinking problem, please think about my story. Don't try to do it by yourself. God knows I tried to control my drinking, telling myself things will get better. Because I was unwilling to seek help outside of myself, I failed. I killed an innocent woman. If anything, I pray to God this story haunts the reader every time he or she gets behind the wheel of a car while impaired.

IN HER OWN WORDS
Allie

I was born into a great and loving family in Northern California, pot country. As much as alcohol was a large part of my substance abuse issues, drugs also played a role in my story. My family loves to drink. Since the day I graduated high school, I was allowed to drink at home as long as I wasn't driving. It's too bad I didn't apply the same rule for myself into adulthood.

I was involved in my first collision at the age of seventeen. Being the well-liked party girl in high school, I had to find a way to have fun and still be able to drive the distance to see my boyfriend after every party. He lived forty-five minutes from my home out in the country. Being a naïve seventeen-year old, I started taking stimulants believing it improved my driving by keeping me alert and awake. My boyfriend, who I had been dating for about six months, did not approve of my new-found habit.

In April 2003, we had been up all-night fighting because he knew I was loaded on stimulants and hadn't slept. I left in the morning and drove to my family's home. I was exhausted due to the lack of sleep. Taking my eyes off the road to change a CD, I over-corrected on a turn and T-boned myself into a couple oak trees. I was pinned in the car for an hour and a half before the paramedics and fire department arrived.

My boyfriend and his roommate also showed up to help. I remember being so scared as I held my boyfriend's hand through the broken sun roof. I was taken by helicopter to the hospital where I learned I had broken my hip, femur, tibia, and fibula bones; basically, I broke my whole left leg. This collision happened a week before my senior prom.

After the collision, I graduated high school and decided to stop using drugs. I continued to drink alcohol because it was much more socially acceptable, especially around my family. With that said, I am an alcoholic and a drug addict.

All I did was simply exchange one substance for another. I received my first driving under the influence (DUI) ticket when I was eighteen years old. Since I was under the legal drinking age I automatically lost my license for a year and was court-ordered to attend Alcoholics Anonymous (A.A.) meetings. About six weeks after my DUI conviction, my boyfriend (the same one who had helped pull me from my collision) died in a tragic dirt bike accident. This event sent me off on a *bender* that went on for years. Deeply in love with that man, I learned the hard lesson of loss at a very difficult time in my life. Now, I took my drinking to a new level.

A year after my boyfriend's death I needed to get out of the small town I had called home for almost twenty years. I decided to move to Southern California and go to college where I was certain the change of scenery and people would help get my life on track. Unfortunately, I took my problems with me, along with the grief I had not dealt with over my boyfriend's death. I became a *full-on maintenance drinker;* beginning when I woke up to whenever I passed out. My anxiety level was very high. I would develop panic attacks that could only be squelched by more booze. I was no longer going to school but drinking daily to calm my nerves enough to feel normal. Originally, I thought I had found nirvana with a bunch of young adults who liked to drink all the way into the morning hours, but I soon discovered being an alcoholic is a very sad, lonely existence.

I hit my bottom in November 2005. It was a couple days before Thanksgiving. I began drinking when I woke up, around ten o'clock in the morning. My friends and I planned to leave the next day to spend the holiday with our respective families. I drank heavily all day. I remember a friend having to support me as I walked home that night. The next morning, I was to drive to Bakersfield to meet with a couple family members and then continue our trip to San Diego for Thanksgiving. I packed my bag the night before and printed the directions. I woke up with anxiety about an hour before

my alarm was set to go off around five o'clock in the morning. I drove an hour and a half thinking that I was totally okay to drive, then I was in a head-on collision.

The morning light was breaking, but it was still mostly dark out as I headed east on a two-line undivided highway with a broken yellow line for passing. The car ahead of me passed the semi-truck that was in front of me. Then I crossed into the left lane to pass the semi-truck. I was about even with the semi-truck when I saw a pair of headlights come up over a hill in the road. I slammed on my brakes to get back behind the semi-truck. The truck driver also slammed on his brakes, so I couldn't get back behind him and out of the oncoming lane in time. I believe the approaching car that was driving in the correct lane slammed on their brakes too. My car hit the oncoming car head-on at about fifty miles per hour (mph).

I remember coming to and being pinned in my car. The front of my car was smashed, fire was coming from the engine, and the car's side window was broken. My first thought was that I needed to get out of the car fast before it exploded. I tried to move but realized I couldn't. I put my hands on my legs and felt the bones popping out. Instantly, I began screaming. A man and his family stopped when they saw the collision. I asked him to please put out the fire in my car. I heard his family yelling at him to leave me in the car as it was going to blow. Somehow that man was able to extinguish the flames.

A lot of the collision is still unclear due to me being in shock. The next thing I remember is seeing a California Highway Patrol (CHP) officer next to me. I also saw a car in front of me that was smashed. I believe I saw an unmoving form in the driver seat. I asked the officer if the other person was okay. He said he wasn't. I lost it. I began screaming again. The officer told me that someone smelled alcohol on my breath and that if I am drunk they are going to charge me with murder. I was then taken by helicopter to the hospital where I was told I had broken both my legs and my lungs were collapsed. I also had a 0.09 blood alcohol concentration (BAC) level from the heavy drinking from the day before.

I spent two weeks in the hospital and six months in a wheel chair as my legs healed. Due to the unsafe road conditions, I was able to plea down to a felony DUI conviction and was sentenced to only one year in jail. I was recently told by my parents that the district attorney actually asked them to sue the state because Highway 46 is such a deadly road. It still needs to be reconstructed so this scenario does not continue to happen. Regardless of that fact, I know in my heart if I wouldn't have been so tired and buzzed from the day before, this collision would have never happened. I took a twenty-six year old man's life. He was on his way to work in the early morning hours. He had two young children and a girlfriend who was following a couple cars behind him that morning and saw the whole horrific collision.

I share the details of this horrific collision because it's real and it happens every fifteen minutes. I wish I could say I quit drinking after the fatal collision, but I didn't. It took me about a year of trying to convince myself this collision was circumstantial and that I wasn't an alcoholic. I failed miserably. Eventually I got sober, but it only lasted for four years the first time. I was very involved in A.A. and spoke at high school *Every 15 Minutes* assemblies against drinking and driving. I also spoke at DUI schools. Eventually I relapsed and as shameful as the collision was, I am just as ashamed to say I did it again one night. About a mile from home, I was pulled over for a missing tail light. I had been drinking in my car shortly before being stopped and had convinced myself that I wouldn't feel the effects of the alcohol until I arrived home.

When I was sober I was adamantly against drinking and driving, but when I picked up an alcoholic beverage, it turns out I didn't stand for anything. That DUI was counted as another felony and with a prior conviction, I served some jail time with a three-year suspended  sentence. I pulled myself together for a while and got some sobriety time behind me. Then I began dating a man and eventually we started using drugs. I violated my probation and ended up serving the three-year suspended sentence at a maximum-security prison in Chowchilla, California.

Prison is an experience I never want to go through ever again. As a drunk driver, you are not looked upon kindly. My freedom and decision-making privledges were taken from me because I couldn't be trusted to make them on my own. I am humbled to say that I deserved to be in prison along with the rest of the murderers. Not only were the choices I made up to that point criminal, but they were fatal. To this day, I believe my sentence was more than warranted.

It has been twelve years since the fatal collision. I am now thirty-three years old. I am clean and sober and lead a life of gratitude. It hasn't always been that way though. I think of the man I killed every day. I think of his family. I wonder why God thought I should live and he should die. I don't lean on alcohol to answer these questions for me anymore. Instead, I try to help people by sharing my story. Honestly, sharing my story allows me to live with myself on a daily basis. There are many people who are serving life sentences for the same crime; yet, I am free. I choose to use my undeserved freedom constructively. There is no sentence that the judge could have handed to me that would ever change what I did. If he could have given me a sentence that would have brought my victim back to life, I would have taken it ten times over.

If there is one thing I hope you can read in my story, know that you should never think this won't happen to you. I thought this sort of thing happened to poor unfortunate souls that had it coming, not to me. But, it did happen to me. You are not immune to alcohol's wrath either. Please hear me now; don't drink and drive. IT COULD HAPPEN TO YOU.

God bless you that it doesn't.

IN HER OWN WORDS
Cari, Founder of Next Step Foundation
Vow to Drive Sober

———

I'm the mom of four beautiful adult children. By the time I was twenty-one years old, I had two girls and a boy. I basically grew up with my first three. At twenty-nine years old, I had another daughter, but that didn't stop me from wanting to be the *cool mom*. I was the mom that allowed my teenagers to drink at home. In fact, when Brandon, my son, turned eighteen years old, which is the legal age to drink in Mexico, I took him there to celebrate his birthday. My two older daughters went with us and it was clearly a *drunkfest*. There was also drinking and driving. Honestly, I don't remember if one of my daughters or I drove, but one of us drove drunk. That wasn't the first or last time I drove drunk with my adult children. I went out with my oldest daughter in a limo when she turned twenty-one years old. We all partied until I was so sick I ended up in the emergency room. When Brandon turned twenty-one years old (I was forty-two years old), we rented a limo for him and his friends to go out to have a good time. Naturally, I went along. Here's our story of how being the *cool mom* can end up causing lifelong extreme guilt.

Brandon was working for our family's small physical therapy neurological clinic as one of our therapy assistants. When Brandon's clients canceled their appointments, he contacted his best friend – it was time for a fun afternoon. When you're twenty-one years old, you feel invincible. Excited for new found freedom and possibilities, you're figuring out who you are as an adult by trying everything. For many, the realization that buzzed driving and drunk driving often comes at a cost.

On a hot, summer day in 2001, Brandon, his best friend and their friend Jessica spent the day hanging out and running errands in Phoenix, Arizona. They were less than a mile from Brandon's apartment, wrapping up their fun, alcohol-filled day together. Brandon was driving Jessica's car with his best friend in the passenger seat and Jessica in the backseat. Driving her car fast, he hit the median, sped into oncoming traffic, and was hit by a full-size truck, a full-size van and a SUV. Brandon and his best friend were airlifted to the nearest trauma hospitals. His best friend was pronounced dead at the hospital. Brandon was in critical condition, suffering from a severe traumatic brain injury with multiple life-threatening injuries and not expected to live. Jessica suffered minor injuries that would heal; however, the emotional injuries are carried with her to this day. Brandon's blood alcohol concentration (BAC) level was 0.14.

I remember walking into Brandon's hospital room and seeing him on life support. He was on death's door. Staff told us that they didn't think he was going to live, and if he did, he would be a vegetable. I was struck with fear and sadness that my son might not live. But, even more fearful that his long-time best friend died because Brandon chose to drive drunk. If Brandon did survive, would he go to jail for manslaughter and would he ever be able to live knowing he killed his best friend?

Months later, Brandon came out of his coma, was taken off life support and began to hold his head up with minimal support. After almost a year of hospitalization, we brought him home. Knowing that I had to provide twenty-four hour care (feeding, bathing, dressing, medication management, bowel care, transportation, etc.) for Brandon and take care of my other family members was overwhelming to say the least. My faith in God is the only thing that got me through this nightmare I seemed to be having; that my son drank, drove, killed his best friend, left Jessica with a life-time of emotional scars and left himself in a completely dependent situation to where I would have to care for him forever.

To this day my faith is what gives me the strength to persevere. After months of working with Brandon to follow simple commands (like lifting his index finger), Arnie, my husband, and I sought out the best rehabilitation facility, and chose one in California. Dedicated to my son's recovery, Brandon and I relocated to California while Arnie and our twelve-year old daughter stayed in Phoenix. This separation intensified the guilt of abandonment that I felt for leaving my young daughter. Aside from short, periodic visits to Phoenix, I spent every day at the clinic with Brandon for eight months.

Realizing Brandon would need daily therapy, Arnie built an extensive, fully-equipped and staffed neurological rehabilitation clinic in 2002. Brandon and I returned to Phoenix the next year to start a new life. I worked at the clinic while Brandon received daily physical, occupational and speech therapy to ensure his continual progress. Surprisingly, it was immensely therapeutic for me to hear our clients' stories, many related to drinking, as well as drinking and driving.

In 2004, Arnie established *The Next Step Foundation*, a nonprofit organization that helps families and athletes with traumatic injuries participate in programs geared toward wellness and recreation. The focus was not, in fact, about drinking and driving due to my guilt of being the cool mom; however, during this time I started calling schools to present our story. Surprisingly, the schools never returned my calls. I didn't call back because in my heart I was terrified of how people would react to our story since it was my son who was the drunk driver, who killed not just anyone, but his best friend.

*Tim Roemer - Left, Cari Fonseca - Right
Brandon Gray - Middle*

Due to the economic recession, Arnie and I had to close the clinic in 2012 after nearly ten years in operation. I knew I had to keep busy after the disappointment of the clinic closing. I started taking Brandon out on walks to pass the time in February 2012. I pushed him in his seventy-five pound wheelchair; Brandon weighed two hundred pounds and I too, was two hundred pounds at the time. We didn't have anything else to do, so I pushed and pushed. Our walking quickly turned into jogging and before I knew what was happening I completed nine miles pushing Brandon.

Now, as an impassioned runner, I decided to run for a cause. My sister suggested we create a team and push Brandon through a full marathon (26.2 miles). I always admired the father/son duo from the Boston Marathon, Dick and Rick

Hoyt. So, to move us further along, I started fundraising for an adult jogging stroller, so Brandon would be more comfortable during the races. We completed our first Arizona Rock 'n' Roll Marathon in January 2013. I pushed him the entire time, which took almost seven hours to complete. Words can't express the emotions I felt when we finished, but my tears said it all. Team Brandon was born.

After three full marathons and a one-half marathon (13.1 miles), I soon realized this was the perfect platform for *Team Brandon* to start sharing our *Vow to Drive Sober* message with the world. *Team Brandon* became the face of *The Next Step Foundation*. To date, *Team Brandon's* speaking engagements have been shared through presentations to schools, worksites and community organizations. This adds up to nearly one hundred presentations to over thirty thousand people of all ages.

Who would have thought the short walks we started in 2012 pushing my six foot, two-hundred pound son would have resulted in completing six full marathons, countless half marathons and many other distance races. By January 2018, we had run over fifty-five hundred miles.

In December 2017, *The Next Step Foundation - Team Brandon* hosted it's inaugural *Vow to Drive Sober 5K / 1 Mile Run, Walk and Wheel Event*. It is an educational event and expo to recognize National Impaired Driving Prevention Month. The lives we touch when we run with our *Vow to Drive Sober* message (printed on the front and back of our neon-yellow shirts) have been seen by hundreds of thousands of people.

Brandon and I have spoken at universities, community colleges, business groups, and middle and high schools. It's especially touching to see the students be so receptive. They thank us for sharing our story and give Brandon hugs and fist bumps. I love getting emails from parents telling me that their son or daughter shared our story with them at dinner. That's when I know we are making a difference!

I know we are doing God's will in helping change the way the world thinks about drinking and driving. *Team Brandon's* goal is to save lives and help others realize the importance of choices. In 2018, we aim to increase the number of schools and organizations that hear our *Vow to Drive Sober* story, which we always share with love and honesty. Because our story is so different, speaking from the offender's point of view, *Team Brandon* is about forgiveness. It's not about pointing a finger in someone's face and saying, "You are a bad person." We all make mistakes. I want people know that choices matter and it's critical to plan ahead. We don't feel that alcohol is the enemy for those over twenty-one years old. Our message is very simple: plan ahead, use alternative transportation, party smart and *Vow to Drive Sober*.

While Brandon didn't go to jail, he is serving a life sentence trapped in his body and mind. Brandon has lost all his friends. He'll never get married, have children, or own a car or house. He's unable to walk, talk, eat or drink, yet he is able to comprehend what is being said and knows that he is helping others make smart choices when it comes to drinking alcohol. I've forgiven myself for being the *cool mom*. I have forgiven Brandon for the poor choice he made that destroyed countless lives. My unconditional love for my family is everlasting; however, I'm still striving to balance the time among all family members, so no one feels like they're taking a back seat to the constant care I need to provide to Brandon.

Since 2001, the financial hardship the crash has put on our family is never-ending. Progress is sometimes a minute-by-minute accomplishment. Our life story is just one reality of impaired driving. Please, friends don't let friends drive drunk. Think before you drink and have a plan. Choices matter! For more information about our story or to watch our video, visit the website at TeamBrandon.org.

IN HER OWN WORDS
DeVyon, A High School Student

When I first saw Brandon at the high school assembly, I envisioned him being able to walk and talk. He is trapped inside of his mind and not able to say the words that he wants to say or hug his family. He is trapped behind an invisible wall. No matter how hard he tries to scream, no one hears him. He sits in solitude listening, waiting, and wanting to be heard. I wrote the following poem from Brandon's perspective.

My Own Personal Purgatory

Trapped mind and soul
From one mistake and it took its toll
The devil's sweet intoxicating elixir on my tongue
Clouded my vision and took over my thoughts
The life that was once so perfect came crashing down like a flying stone to glass
The damage the sweet elixir caused me to do did not leave me nor anyone else unharmed
And as a punishment I stay bounded to the body that I once loved now my prison
The person that I once was I can no longer be
I now sit in this husk of a body
Aware of my surroundings but not able to make a sound
I, My body, And form is the price for the mistake I made
And for the friend I lost
And so I tell my story to so many people to urge you
To warn you
To make you aware
And so that you don't make the same mistake I did
Because of the Devil's sweet intoxicating elixir on my lips
And the punisher of my deeds

IN HIS OWN WORDS
Gerardo

My name is Gerardo. I was born in El Salvador during a civil war. My fifteen year old single mother raised me alone since my father left us when I was two months old. He left the country because of the war and never came back.

For the first six years of my life I remember being abused, both verbally and physically by my mother and neighbors. By the age of eleven, I asked questions like, "Why does my mom hate me so much?" I could understand the reasons my neighbors treated me badly, but not my mother. When I turned eleven years old I wanted to learn a profession in order to get a job that would help to support the family, as we were very poor. By the age of seventeen, I became a mechanic and was introduced to alcohol. At first, I didn't like it until I noticed that the pain and emotions I felt towards my mother were smoothed over. Alcohol seemed to heal my wounds.

I then left my country and came to the United States of America. At first, I didn't like it and I used alcohol every time I became depressed. In 1999, I received my first driving under the influence (DUI) conviction, so I stopped drinking for the next six months. It wasn't until the next depression hit that I began to drink again to numb the pain of the memories of my mother and the evil neighbors. I started to hate myself too.

In 2005, I was drunk and involved in an auto collision that killed an innocent person. I was sentenced

Jim Sullivan/J. Sullivan Productions

to fifteen years to life in prison. By 2008, I was completely suicidal. Right at the same time, I fortunately discovered God while some real good friends talked me out of suicide.

They got me involved in self-help groups and for the first time, I opened up my heart. I discovered that the resentment I held toward my mother and the neighbors was a big reason as to why I drank. By 2013, I learned to forgive the people who hurt me, including my mother. It was very hard for me, I couldn't understand why she hated me so much. Why did she abuse me? I came to realize that she did what she knew based on her experience. I realized she worked since she was just a little girl and suffered a hard life. I felt so bad the day I understood she raised me the same way she was raised. It was one of the worst feelings I had experienced in my entire life. All those years I thought my mom hated me, so she abused me. I came to the realization that I LOVE MY MOM and she loved me and did the best she could for me!

I was the first one in my family with a life sentence. I figured I had two choices: 1) get an education, regardless of the obstacles, or 2) continue my life as I knew it on the street – drinking alcohol and doing drugs. Thanks to Narcotics Anonymous (NA), Alcoholics Anonymous (A.A.), and some other groups I joined, I realized that I had a sickness and was hurting all the people who believed in me and loved me. Thanks to God, I made a change in my life. I learned to read and write the English language and earned my General Education Diploma (GED). I also learned a vocational trade – Auto Body. I started to feel good about myself without alcohol.

I've been in prison for ten years. Since 2008, I have tried to be the best role model for my son and my family. As a family man, I'm now preparing to marry a beautiful Christian lady whom I love so much. I can now see the next ten years as a blessing: married with two children, a boy and a girl. I dream of having my own auto body shop and offering drug and alcohol counseling to as many people as possible. I give thanks to the men who poured their hearts into me and helped me become the man I am today. They were a blessing to me in so many ways. In order for me to achieve my dreams, I must keep pushing forward. I thank God for giving me a second chance.

IN HIS OWN WORDS
Mark

I was born in 1955 in California into a loving Christian family. In our home, cocktail hour was part of our everyday evening meal. I started drinking and partying at an early age. Back in those days, the laws were not as strict as they are today, and many people didn't think twice about having a drink or two and driving home.

After graduating from high school, I started working in construction. This was an especially a good place to find fellow drinkers. I was a foreman and a heavy equipment operator for an asphalt company. At the end of the day when everyone returned to the shop, the boss would pay for a case of beer. We would all have a few beers before heading home. In those days, I was arrested a few times for driving under the influence (DUI) but most of the time, I just paid the fine and it was done.

No one else in my family had ever been arrested, and I probably wouldn't have either, if it was not for my addiction to partying. You see, I always wanted to be the cool guy. I never thought I had a problem. I was in denial. I thought I was doing so well. I had a nice house, a new car, a good job, and a totally hot babe living with me. Everything was good until one day after work when I was driving home on a two-lane highway. I had a couple beers and stopped to pick up a burger. I decided to eat it on the way home. This was another bad choice. Now, I was under the influence of alcohol and distracted driving. As I ate the good-sized hamburger while driving at fifty-five miles per hour (mph), part of the burger suddenly fell into my lap. I remember thinking, "What next?"

I glanced down to pick up the mess in my lap and took my eyes off the road. It was long enough to drift into the oncoming lane of traffic. I struck an oncoming car head-on. It was a horrific collision, from which would take me years to recover. This crash happened in 1986, thirty-two years ago. There were three fatalities. I know as a Christian, God has forgiven me for this terrible tragedy, but for many years, those murders have haunted me. It took a very long time and years in recovery to forgive myself.

My blood alcohol level was 0.04, and I was sentenced to six years in prison for vehicular manslaughter. A person doesn't need to be drunk in order to cause a horrific collision. The combination of a little alcohol and a distraction can be deadly!

After I was released from prison, I stopped drinking because of the guilt I felt. I started working in the construction trade again. About twenty years ago some of my fellow co-workers, who are truckers, were talking to me about the dangers of alcohol and driving. They said, "Don't drink anymore." They told me they use speed instead because it keeps them alert, especially when driving long days. Speed sounded great because I never wanted to experience another horrific crash like what I experienced before. I justified this newfound addiction as perfectly safe because it kept me alert. In the end, I had given up alcohol only to replace it with another addictive substance. I found out later this was a big mistake.

Drunk driving, buzzed driving or distracted driving; it's all the same. That includes texting and driving. Even if I had no alcohol in my system the day of my crash, I believe that in the

short amount of time I had to react before I drifted into the other lane, I still would not have been able to avoid the auto collision.

As I drove home one evening in 2005, I was *pulled over* for having a burned-out brake light on the cab of my truck. The officer spotted a ten-dollar baggie of speed in my truck, so I was arrested. I also tested positive for a controlled substance. I posted bail for $8,000 and was released. I missed my court date and a warrant for my arrest was issued. Needless to say, the judge was more than just a little *pissed off* and during the trial he accused me of thumbing my nose at the law. I was convicted for possession and being under the influence of a controlled substance. Combined with my prior manslaughter conviction from 1986 (I received a strike for each fatality), I was sentenced under California's three strikes law.

The judge felt I disregarded the law and needed to be taught a lesson, so instead of giving me one strike for the prior prison term and doubling my current sentence, the judge struck me out and sentenced me to twenty-five years to life for two minor drug offenses. This is no joke. It can happen to you too. I was given an additional twenty-five years to life sentence for failure to appear in court. This type of sentencing is allowed under California's three strikes law. The two sentences were to run consecutive making my current sentence a total of fifty years to life.

I am now serving a life sentence for offenses most people consider minor offenses. Don't be fooled. This is serious. I started my sentence at one of the worst Level Four yards in California. The people in the yard are not low-level drug offenders like me. They are hardcore. I have been clean and sober thirteen years now, and I have been involved in numerous substance abuse and rehabilitation programs, especially Celebrate Recovery, where I have served as a facilitator for the past six years. I continually make amends to those I have hurt by my reckless actions by helping others with *their* rehabilitation. Although I am currently serving time in a California prison, I have found peace. I pray my testimony may help someone reach out for help before it is too late. Just maybe a life can be saved.

IN HIS OWN WORDS
Peter B.

I joined the Marines after I graduated high school. I went through nine months of training. I was sober the whole time, but always felt like drinking (I started drinking alcohol at the age of twelve). I wanted to smoke marijuana but knew that we get random drug tests in the Marines, so I did not want to risk my career. In 2006, I was stationed at the Marine Corps Logistics Base Barstow as a Military Police Officer. Some of the marines I worked with invited me to a BBQ. Everyone was drinking, and I wanted to drink but I was under age. Then my corporal came to me and asked why I wasn't drinking? I told him, "Because I am nineteen." He went to the ice chest and grabbed two beers and gave them to me.

After that day, my alcoholism significantly progressed to almost daily drinking. Like other Marines, I entertained the excuse, "I was in the middle of the desert with nothing to do but drink." I thought if I am willing to risk my life for my country, I deserve to drink a beer. The problem with that thinking was it wasn't only a beer, it was a lot of beers. I had an unjustified sense of entitlement. Serving my country does not mean I can violate the laws of the country.

One day, I received a call from a corporal who told me to report in because I was being investigated for underage drinking. I violated the California Vehicle Code and the rules and regulations of the Marine Corps, so I was subject to Non-Judicial-Punishment (NJP). I was charged with underage drinking, driving under the influence, dereliction of duty, and disobeying a lawful order. At the NJP hearing, I reported to the 1st Sgt where he told me that they violated my Article 31 rights (Miranda Rights) and that the charges against me are dropped. He told me that it was a shame that I couldn't wait until my twenty-first birthday to drink. He also told me that I got away this time.

About a year and a half later I received a call from a girl

to come over to her house. As I drove to her house, I received a phone call and pulled over on the side of the freeway. As I talked on the phone, a California Highway Patrol (CHP) officer pulled up behind me. I threw all the empty cans in the back seat as the CHP officer approached my vehicle. He told me to step out of the car and then had me perform a Field Sobriety Test (FST), and blow into the Preliminary Alcohol Screening (PAS) device. I knew that I was going to get a DUI because I knew I had drank a lot and was feeling buzzed. He asked me if I knew what the legal limit was, and I told him, "Yes, 0.08." Then he showed me the PAS device and it read .078. I was so happy and started yelling, "YES!" I was jumping up and down on the side of the freeway knowing that I wasn't going to be arrested for a DUI. The CHP officer then gave me the plastic mouth piece and told me, "Take this to remember the day you got away." I took it and put it in my center console.

On another occasion, I drove up a hill in a fifty-five mile per hour (mph) zone going one-hundred mph. I soon noticed a Los Angeles County Sheriff behind me and when I reached the bottom of the hill he pulled me over. He opened my car door, took off my seat belt, yanked me out of my car and slammed me on the hood of his patrol car. He then searched me, handcuffed me, and put me in the back seat of his car. He searched my car and ran my information on his computer. He asked me if liked driving fast and I said, "Yes." He also asked me if I have been drinking and I told him, "Yes". He asked me if I was a marine and I said, "Yes." Then, he opened the car door and told me to get out. He took off the handcuffs and said to me, "Go before you do something stupid." Instead of looking at this incident as a close call and that I should have been arrested for driving under the influence (DUI) again, I ended up bragging on how I got away. As a Military Police Officer, I always felt that I was above the law. I drove fast, drank alcohol and drove, and drank while driving just because I thought I could get away with it and that nothing will happen to me.

I never thought that I would get a DUI. It would happen to other people or my friends but not me. I always felt that it was okay for me to drive drunk, but that was false. One day, I pulled into a parking lot, so my friend could get the weed out of the car trunk. When I pulled into the parking lot I hit a tree going thirty-five mph. A CHP officer watched me the whole time. He told me to get out of the car and he started his FST.

Then he had me blow into the PAS device. I blew a 0.18. I was double over the legal limit, consequently, he arrested me for a DUI. He released my friend because he was not injured. He walked home.

My car was totaled, but I did pay to get it out of the impound. Eventually, I went to court and plead no contest to DUI. The judge ordered that my license be suspended for one year, placed me on three-years' summary probation, and ordered me to pay a fine, to serve twelve days of community service, and to complete a three-month DUI program. This was a big inconvenience to me because I had to drive eighty-six miles one way to get to work. The DUI course that I attended was a joke and I learned nothing. The counselor's attitude: since none of us wanted to be in class, let's make the best of it by watching movies. I was relieved after I completed the course. To me, it was a waste of time.

I also attended Alcoholics Anonymous meetings, which I hated. I thought they were full of a bunch of weirdos. I know now that I was supposed to learn a lot of things, unfortunately, I didn't take it seriously either. If my attitude would have been better, I might have learned something. Now, I attend Alcoholics Anonymous and have learned the steps. I wish that I would have taken Alcoholics Anonymous more seriously outside of prison. It probably would have prevented me from a lot of heartache.

After my DUI, I didn't want to drink or drive. I was afraid to get behind the wheel again. My desire to drink was gone. But then I started hanging around people who drank, soon I was right back to my old habits. Shortly before I was discharged from the Marine Corps I started smoking marijuana again. I didn't care about the consequences. Then, I tried cocaine. I liked how it made me feel. I felt strong and energetic. It made me aggressive and I liked that feeling. By this time, I was using drugs and alcohol to cope with the stress of relationship problems, depression, anger, and frustration. It was my way of dealing with life's problems, but all I did was compound them.

Out of the Marine Corps I started attending raves and experimenting with ecstasy, acid, and mushrooms. My life began to spin out of control as I was always chasing a high. I finally realized that my life was in a downward spiral. I decided to re-enlist in the Marine Corps and I slowly eliminated my use of drugs. In January 2011, after going to a rave, I decided that this day would be the last day I did any drugs. However, I was still going to drink alcohol. I never sought help to try to get sober and I did it all on my own, but I didn't fully acknowledge the drug and alcohol problem that I had.

In January 2011, my best friend Alice invited me to go to a party with her. I went to the grocery store and bought some whiskey and soda pop. I invited my friend Job to join me. We arrived at Alice's house, kicked back, but soon became bored. I received an invitation to another party and asked Job, Alice, and Kerri if they wanted to go to the other party. They said, "Yes."

While I drove, my friend Job sat in the front passenger seat, Kerri sat in the back seat on the driver's side, and Alice sat in the back seat on the passenger's side. As I was speeding down the freeway, a car cut in front of me. I swerved to the left to avoid a crash. I drove fast. Kerri asked me to slow down. I did, but I missed the on ramp. I was texting a message. When I finished the message, I looked up and there was a fork in the road. I was going about one-hundred mph in a forty mph zone. I steered the car to the right, but didn't make it. I ran off the road and nearly missed a statue in a park.

Wyoming Governor's Council on Impaired Driving

My car went air borne and started to roll. As the car rolled I hit a tree on the passenger side where Alice sat. My car rolled several more times, striking multiple trees. I was knocked unconscious. When I woke up my car was resting on the passenger side. I unbuckled my seat belt and got out of the car. I went toward the sunroof and a bystander and I tore it off, so I could help Job out. I discovered that Job was unconscious and shook him until he woke up. I took off his seat belt and he started yelling in pain, so I didn't move him. Once I knew he was alright I went to find Alice and Kerri. I looked through the back window which was missing and saw no one. I started to worry because I could not find them. Behind me I heard a girl crying. I turned around and saw Kerri under a tree. I still could not find Alice.

Thinking only of me, I asked Job to say that he was the driver because I didn't want to be in trouble for another DUI. He replied, "No." I could hear in the distance police, fire department, and ambulance sirens coming. The ambulance came and placed me on a gurney. I heard one of the medics say, "We have a fatality". My heart sank and asked who it was. They said that they didn't know, but it was a girl. I knew then that Alice had died. She was partially ejected out of the car and half her body was pinned underneath the car. The emotions I felt were sorrow, guilt, and anger all rolled into one.

The sorrow, because my best friend was killed. The guilt, because my best friend was killed because of me. I was angry at myself for letting this collision happen. I hated myself for being so stupid, irresponsible, selfish, and careless. Thoughts of trading places with my friend Alice ran through my mind. I said to myself that I would rather have died than her. I deserved it. I then remembered the plastic mouth piece that the CHP officer gave me. It was still in my car console. I remembered what he said, "Take this to remember the day you got away." This time I did not get away and my friend Alice died because of my choice to drink and drive.

At the hospital I asked the police officer what my charges would be and he told me Second Degree Murder. My heart sank. I couldn't believe that I was being charged with murder. A few days later I started having thoughts of suicide. I had just lost the will to live and the guilt of killing my friend weighed heavily on me. I later found out in court the extent of everyone else's injuries. Job broke his collarbone, had lacerations on his face and head, split his chin which required stitches, had a black eye, developed blood clots in his lungs, and sustained a concussion. Kerri injured her knee that required fourteen stitches, had bruising on her face and arms, developed neck and back pain, and she sustained a concussion. I fractured my tailbone, had an aneurysm and sustained a concussion. Alice had multiple traumatic injuries. She fractured her second rib, left clavicle, right arm, and right squamous temporal bone. She also had lacerations, and contusions, and sustained external blunt force trauma, which ultimately resulted in her death.

The District Attorney's (DA) opening statement stated, "This case is about someone who thinks the rules do not apply to him, someone who thinks he can get away with disregarding the law, someone who knows the dangers that he's creating but takes the risk anyway. It's about creating a dangerous situation and consciously disregarding a known risk at the cost of other people's lives. We are all here because in the early morning hours of January XX, 2011, the defendant, Peter B., killed twenty-one year old Alice because of a number of reckless choices that he made." At the time the DA was saying this I didn't believe she was speaking the truth, but looking back, now I realize that every word she said was true. I was convicted of Second Degree Murder and sentenced to fifteen years to life in prison.

    I write my story so that you, the reader, know that drinking alcohol and driving is never an option. People can and will be killed as a result of this action. You may think that it will never happen to you, but it CAN. I had the same thought. As you can tell by my life story, it did happen to me. My best friend did not deserve to die. She had a right to live, but I took that from her. Buzzed driving is drunk driving. I felt buzzed that night and I didn't believe that I was drunk. Texting while driving can also have the same result. Texting led me to take my eyes off the road. You not only endanger innocent people's lives, but also the ones you love.

    Value your life and the lives of others. Don't get behind the wheel when you have been drinking. It is not worth it. I would do anything to have my friend back, to not suffer the guilt I have, and to not put a burden on my family. You not only affect your life, but those that love you the most, your family. You bring heartbreak to the victim's family. Margaret lost her sister on her birthday. For the rest of Margaret's life, she will be reminded of her sister's death. Instead of her birthday being a joyous event she will have the pain of remembering the day her sister died.

    I have hurt and caused pain and sorrow to many people, over something that is one-hundred percent preventable. I ask you to have the courage to not drink and drive. I hope and pray that my story has helped you realize the depth of your choices. Drinking and driving is never worth it. It's never an option. The cost is greater that you can ever imagine.

IN HER OWN WORDS
Jennifer, American Family Insurance Agent

I'm sitting in front of two very kind people. I don't know them. I have never met them and my stomach is in knots. Something isn't right. This is not a conversation I want to be having. They aren't even my clients. He begins to talk, and I become nauseous. I feel raw. I want to fix this for them, but nothing can be done.

Tears can't be held back anymore as they tell me about Anita and her granddaughter Kate. It was a Monday evening and they were on their way home from work when they were hit head-on by a drunk driver. The car was totaled. Kate is on life support. Anita is dead. Dead! I'm f****ing angry at some nameless drunk. A drunk who selfishly took the life of a dear client who was nothing but gentle, hardworking, and thoughtful.

Anita's brother flew into town from out of state. He is physically in my office, but his mind is at a loss. It feels as though he is looking to me for either comfort or confirmation of Anita's death. Trying to wrap his head around what has happened, he asks what the auto policy covers as if he is trying to make small talk to cover up how devastating it truly is to have this conversation.

There is a very small death benefit amount of $5,000 per person attached to the auto policy. I am feeling disgusted as I explain the small amount of money they get in exchange for such a gross loss. This conversation feels wrong on so many levels. I offer my support – give them my personal contact information and beg them to call if there is anything I can do to help.

A week later, the brother returns to my office. He tearfully tells me Kate, an honors student in her senior year of college, was taken off life support. Kate is dead. Dead!

Anger toward the nameless drunk overwhelms me again. How dare he steal not just Anita's life, but now the future of a young woman with big dreams? It hurts me that so much has been taken from this family, and there is nothing I can do to fix these senseless deaths. My career is based on protecting my client's assets. Life is the most important asset and to experience a life lost really hurts, especially since it is completely out of my control.

Sadly, this isn't the first drunk driver story I have experienced during my career as an insurance agent. It is by far the worst. These losses are not only felt by the families' who have a direct loss, but also by every other driver. All drivers are paying for these losses through their high insurance premiums.

Assuming the drunk driver *has insurance*, he or she will probably be dropped from his or her insurance company. If the person can find another company to insure them, he or she is looking at a dramatic increase in the premiums. The drunk can't hide. If the driver shares an address with another person who is insured, insurance companies are so technologically advanced that they will be able to see other drivers in the home and ask about them. Even if the impaired driver *doesn't drive or doesn't have a car,* insurance companies will want to rate him or her or exclude them from insurance coverage, if the person's name appears in a household.

More than likely the impaired driver will have to go to jail, lose his job, and eventually, when allowed to drive again, the state will require proof of insurance via an SR-22 (this may vary by state), which is costly for the impaired driver.

Typically, the drunk driver will have to get a breathalyzer device installed in his/her car. This is another big expense. Most states require the person to rent the breathalyzer device and then have them calibrated periodically. All this costs more and more money.

If the driver *doesn't have* insurance, which to be frank, is often the case in drunk driving crashes, the uninsured motorist coverage of the victim will take care of bodily injury as a result of the collision. Drivers pay attention:

Coverage of the victim's vehicle should be paid by the at-fault drunk driver's insurance. However, if the drunk driver didn't have insurance, the victim will end up having to pay! If the victim had collision coverage, the victim will have to pay the deductible and the insurance company may or may not attempt to subrogate the physical damage, loss of the vehicle and hopefully return the deductible to the victim.

> **The cost can be expensive, ranging from an average premium increase of 12% to 321% depending on your state. The average cost of car insurance with a DUI is $2,143.**
>
> *Insurance.com*

If the victim doesn't have collision coverage and the drunk driver doesn't have any or enough insurance to cover the damage, the victim will be out of pocket for all of the physical damage to the car.

Each time there is a crash, whether it is fatal or not, it is noted by the Department of Motor Vehicles and shared with each state. The more crashes that occur within a certain area, the higher the premiums everyone in that area will pay.

Losses due to fatal car crashes are often shared through premium increases that all drivers pay year after year. Granted, rating calculations vary by company and there are many considerations beyond drunk drivers that affect insurance rates; however, gross accidents, especially those that involve a death(s), will be felt by many, whether the public knows it or not.

Add up the cost of court, jail time, job loss, increased insurance premiums, the cost of a SR-22, deductibles, repairs, lawsuits, attorney fees, plus the agony of living with oneself for the death of an innocent person who happened to be in the right place, but wrong time.

After adding up the costs of a DUI conviction (let alone the possible loss of life) it is hard to imagine why any person who drinks too much alcohol would not call a ride-share company or a taxi to drive them home after a night (or day) of drinking. The price of the extra drinks alone would pay for their safe transportation. Nothing, especially a few more drinks at a bar, is worth the risk of the loss of life!

IN HIS OWN WORDS
Sergio

I was behind the wheel right after I had been drinking too much. My girlfriend sat at the passenger's side and Elisa sat in the back seat, right behind my girlfriend. I put my seatbelt on and started our drive home. However, I didn't pay attention if they had buckled their seatbelts. As I drove, I looked at the fuel gauge. When I returned my eyes to the road, a curve was directly ahead. I immediately broke very hard; the truck started going sideways, hitting the side of the curve. We rolled over and the truck rested on the passenger's side.

Immediately I asked my girlfriend, "Are you okay?"

She replied, "I'm okay."

Then I called for Elisa, "Are you okay?" There was no answer. I quickly took my seatbelt off and looked in the back seat trying to find her, but she wasn't there. I climbed through the driver's side window and went to look for Elisa. I found her lying on the ground face up next to the truck. I thought she was unconscious because there was no blood or scratches visible on her body. Instinctively I slapped her cheek a couple of times and continued to ask her if she was okay. I received no answer.

While I was trying to bring my friend back to consciousness, I heard my girlfriend calling from inside the truck saying, "Where is Elisa? What's going on?"

Because the pick-up truck was resting on the passenger side she was unable to get out of it. Feeling desperate and tense, my heart rate increased as I realized that the crash was very bad. I ran toward the truck and broke the back window in order to get my girlfriend out. As soon as she was out we returned to where Elisa laid. We started administering first aid, but our attempts to wake her up didn't work. She didn't respond, but she was breathing. By now, it was dark outside and there were no street lights in the area. No one was around to ask for help because we were on a desolate road.

I called my best friend (J), but the phone signal was poor. After several attempts the call went through. I told him that I had crashed and needed his help. I told him the location of the crash, and that I was f***ed-up. He didn't hesitate at my request. It took him fifteen minutes to arrive.

Upon his arrival, I asked him to help me to take Elisa to the hospital. He answered, "We can't move her, we have to get help." I became scared to think of the possible consequences. The fear of facing Law Enforcement and Elisa's family.

The thought of fleeing from the crime crossed my mind at that point, but my friend (J) didn't want to move her. He suggested I go to the closest city to get help. The thoughts of fleeing became more real. I told my girlfriend that my friend (J) and I must go to town to get help. I asked her if she would stay with Elisa, to which she answered crying, "Yes, I will stay with her." My friend and I drove away in his truck. Approximately five-hundred meters from the scene I dialed 911. The call went through and I gave them a fake name and hung-up.

As we entered the city limits, I received a phone call from my girlfriend telling me that Elisa wasn't breathing, and she had died. That was the worst news I had ever received. Feeling completely hopeless and scared, my idea of fleeing, now became a choice and a reality. At the first stop sign, I got out of my friend's truck and ran. I headed toward the border and spent the rest of the night in a hotel room in Mexico.

Thoughts of what happened and the idea of calling friends and family members were *running through my mind at a hundred miles an hour.* I could not believe what I had just done. I had taken Elisa's life. My intent for the phone calls was to get financial help to continue fleeing. Some of the people I called agreed to provide me help, while some did not. Even with the help, I questioned myself, "Was it the right thing to flee and to continue running for the rest of my life?" "How could I have left Elisa dying in the desert with my girlfriend by her side?" I had no answer for my actions in that moment. I made another call, this time to my sister. I told her everything that had happened and what I had done. She told me that I could not continue running. I needed to take responsibility for my actions. I needed to face the consequences like a man.

Besides, Elisa's family deserved that I take responsibility.

My sister told me that I had to turn myself in and that she would be there for me. She helped me realize that I had to do the right thing and turn myself in to the authorities; and I did. When I turned myself into the police, they handcuffed me. In that moment, I realized that running was not a good decision.

In jail I asked myself, "How did all this happen? Elisa is dead and I'm in jail." It took me several years to answer this question. At this point in my life, I believe I have an answer. This life-ending and changing event isn't the result of merely one night of drinking and driving, but it is the result of a collection of unresolved issues and maladaptive behaviors that I developed throughout my life.

The first change I made while incarcerated was to stop drinking alcohol, even though I had no insight into my alcoholism. I had made a commitment to myself, not to drink anymore. Why? Because of my irresponsible drinking and faulty decisions, I killed my friend, devastated her family, and made my family, my girlfriend, and many other people suffer too. Of course, I was in jail facing murder charges too. The effects of my actions were much more, but at the time that was all I could see and what kept me from drinking. I didn't consider myself an alcoholic nor did I think that I was dependent on alcohol. In my distorted view, I thought that an alcoholic was a person who would drink until he/she would end up on the floor, wasted, and sleeping under a bridge.

My point of view, I wasn't that person. The reality, I was reluctant to accept my alcohol dependency. Even though I was aware of the pain and damage that I had caused on account of my drinking, I was still under the belief that I could treat my alcohol dependency as a superficial thing by just *stopping*. I was in denial.

I was sentenced to fifteen years to life in prison. Once incarcerated, I had the opportunity to attend self-help groups. I received my GED certificate. I enrolled in college and studied business and auto-tech courses. With seven years served, I was still abstinent but there were no significant changes in my way of thinking or feeling.

One day I received a visit from someone very special to me; my mother. I had not seen her in eleven years. I was excited and happy as I finally got to see my mother again. I was expecting to see my mother just as she looked the last time I saw her. What a surprise. When I saw her face she had aged; she had more face marks and walked slowly. In that moment I realized that I was still doing damage to others, even without drinking.

I didn't want to do any more damage to my mother, family, or other people. I realized that a good son does not cause such a pain to his mother. I will never forget those thoughts and feelings until my dying day. After visiting with my mother, I became motivated to be a good son, brother, friend, student, and person. In other words, change. This internal motivation to change and be a better person made me commit myself to seek all types of help to better myself.

I attended various self-help groups and classes: spiritual, healthy lifestyle, continuing college (especially Alcohol and Drug Studies courses), and vocational training. I read inspirational books. I wanted to be a better person, to be honest, in peace, and good with myself. I humbly asked God to help me to change and to be a better person. I then began to work on what I considered my most valuable discovery. I began to know myself.

I caused irreversible damage because I killed Elisa. I took everything from her: memories, dreams, the opportunity of being a mother, a professional (psychologist), and having her own family. Also, I caused her family great emotional, mental, physical, and economic damage, which caused them to live with suffering, trauma and life without Elisa. I changed their lives forever.

The damage I caused my ex-girlfriend was significant too. I traumatized her when I left her with Elisa as she was dying in that dark and desolate place. It was my responsibility to take her and Elisa safely back to their home. I also caused damage to my friend by involving him in a difficult situation as he tried to help me. He could have been seriously traumatized by my decision to run. My family has suffered the consequences of my actions because of the emotional and financial problems and the shame they live with daily. Lastly, during all the time of my alcohol abuse I was on a path of self-destruction. Recognizing the damage, pain, shame, remorse, and sadness that I caused to so many people, became the reasons for me to continue changing.

Later in my recovery process I was able to see the correlation between my alcohol dependency and the significant childhood events that I experienced (illness, my mother's overprotection, and my father's negligence), and the resulting issues (inferiority complex, emotional constriction, dependent personality, loneliness, depression, arrogance, selfishness, impulsiveness, irresponsibility, insecurity, self-defeating thoughts of worthlessness, being different and weak). Alcohol became my remedy to self-medicate all of these issues. Due to the self-exploration and reflection I learned, and still am learning, my alcohol dependency was (is) an internal rather than external issue. Therefore, I had to search for solutions, specifically aimed toward my internal thoughts instead of alcohol use. I started by questioning my core beliefs of who I am. I concluded that I wasn't the person I thought I was and began to replace the negative thoughts with appropriate positive ones.

Eventually, I saw that I am a person with many strengths such as a strong faith in God and being connected to a good family and friends who love me. This new way of thinking was, for me, as if I had rewired my brain. As I was changing my way of thinking and learning skills to deal with my feelings, I was also changing my behavior, character, and adopting positive habits such as attending church regularly, praying, meditating, caring for others, developing positive relationships, continuing my education, attending self-help groups, exercising, sleeping well, and practicing good nutrition.

At the same time, this new way of thinking helped me to work through my emotions, gaining autonomy, tolerating stress, and having a more appropriate perspective of life. As a result, I gradually became a more optimistic, hopeful, and resilient (ability to bounce back from adversity) person. Only then was I able to see that one's thoughts, feelings, and behaviors are related. I also learned that by accepting and treating my alcohol dependency I gain control over it, instead of being controlled by it.

With this new way of thinking, feeling, and behaving, I was able to see myself and the world with a new perspective. I recognized that instead of causing so much damage to people and myself, as I had done in the past; now I was capable of doing good and helping others. I began helping others any way I could, especially with those who needed help with their alcohol dependency. As I helped, I benefited as it reinforced my sobriety and motivated me to becoming a productive person. Now I accept and love myself. Not in the selfish way, but in a confident way, so I can love others as well.

Reflecting on all the damage and pain that I caused, due my maladaptive behaviors, I now realize that it was necessary for me to come to prison, so I would not damage more people. Being in prison has strengthened me. Unfortunately, Elisa had to die in order for me to change. I will have that in mind until my dying day.

I would like to mention that my personal choice to trust God and to have a strong relationship with Him is a base for my rehabilitation process. Nonetheless, I am responsible to treat my alcohol dependency for the rest of my life, one day at a time. I have learned that life is a succession of moments and made by decisions, either good or bad. Now, besides feeling good, at peace, and being sober, I have found my purpose in life (things that I would like to do for the rest of my life) – to help others rehabilitate, have my own family, and to work on the oil rigs again. At the same time, I have hope, optimism, energy, excitement, and confidence. By being sober, healed, and in tune with my authentic self, whether in prison or in the free community, I finally feel free.

I believe that if I could change, having had so many issues. I believe anybody has the capacity to change and to live with dignity, respect, peace, and joy, if they choose.

We are born to love, we live to love, and we will die to love still more.
St. Joseph Cafasso

IN HIS OWN WORDS
Brian

    It started as a crisp, sunny March day a few months before my eighteenth birthday. Although the day seemed like any other day, little did I know it would be the last day for one of my close friends; I caused it. We planned on hanging out that night by chilling at my pad with a twelve-pack of beer. Of course, as the day progressed, our plans changed. I was *cool* with the change, More friends and a different location.

    I lived about seven miles out of town in a mobile home park. It was located down a dangerous winding road that most people stayed away from if they lived elsewhere in town. It was a small community and a fun place to grow up during my teenage years. I got into quite a bit of trouble with my handful of friends. We were always hanging out or partying as much as we could. Before school, after school, and of course on the weekends. It's safe to say that I was *messed up* one way or another the majority of my high school days.

    I started smoking weed and drinking alcohol at the age of thirteen, and smoking cigarettes at the age of fifteen. I tried crystal meth on my sixteenth birthday and was addicted to a prescription pain medicine by the last half of my sixteenth year. At seventeen years old, I was smoking weed and a pack of cigarettes daily, getting blackout drunk two to three times a week, and taking Ecstasy pills every other weekend. At about seventeen and a half years old, my lifestyle got worse: bigger parties, more drugs, new people, and new influences. One week I tried cocaine, acid, mushrooms and some weird hallucinogenic pills all for the first time. All this took place within a week before my horrific collision. I guess it was God's way of teaching me a lesson.

    My buddy, Sam just got off work and came over to my pad to pick me up so we could go to a party. My parents were easy going and all my friends got along with them. After hanging out for a few minutes, we left my house and drove into town to meet up with a group of friends. There were seven friends, and one friend was over twenty-one years old. That was our main reason to meet them at a convenience store. I just wanted to get drunk and party. Sam, Tom and I had an eighteen-pack of beer to share while the others got their own beer and a bottle of whiskey. We decided on a place to chill and started driving in that direction. Ready to party.

The party spot happened to be past my house, further down the winding road. It was a dead end; a perfect little area except that there was a property beyond a gate at the dead end. We didn't care, so we opened the car doors, turned up the radio and started partying. We drank a couple of beers and smoked some of the weed I had brought. We chilled for about an hour. Talking, laughing, listening to music and enjoying the mountains and open night sky. A few cars drove through the gate to the property, so we decided it might be smart to find somewhere else to party in case the property owner didn't want us near their house. This location was known for underage drinking and we didn't want the cops to be called, so we decided that it was time to go.

Up to this point Sam had been driving his car. It didn't have a radio and was smaller than my car, so we decided to change vehicles and use mine instead. We were buzzed and wanted music and more leg and head-room to move around, so I volunteered myself and my four-wheel vehicle. It was bigger, faster and had a new stereo system. Perfect! We had to pass by my house on the way to the next place anyway, so why not. We took off and stopped by my place. I already had the keys in my pocket so a couple guys and I pushed my vehicle out of its parking spot and down the road about thirty yards. I started it there so my parents wouldn't hear the ignition start and come out asking questions. I turned the music on, turned it up, got everyone in, and took off. Down the road we went.

By this time, I had a buzz and my driving reflected it. I sped out of the mobile home park down the winding road. The SUV that followed struggled to keep up and the driver was more messed up than me. At the bottom of the hill the road took a sharp turn to the left, which I maneuvered, but the other driver didn't. She lost traction and side swiped a large boulder, which tore up the whole passenger side of the vehicle. We didn't stop there.

We continued driving. It was her mom's car anyway, so I

didn't care. We drove straight through town to the opposite side and down a dark road up into an upcoming housing development that was in the middle of construction. There were only a couple of houses around and it was up in the hills away from everything; nice and quiet. We parked up by a water tower, opened the doors, turned up the music and continued on partying the night away.

After a couple more beers, I picked up a bottle of whiskey. I wasn't planning on drinking too much, but I figured, "What the hell, why not? One shot won't kill me." So I took a chug. The bottle was passed around and I ended up with it again. I took a couple more chugs. I was feeling pretty good. I had all the confidence in the world, especially behind the wheel of a car.

It was close to two o'clock in the morning and we decided to put an end to the night. Some of us were buzzed, some of us were just plain drunk. I was somewhere in the middle of being buzzed and drunk. I decided I was fine to drive, so four people (two of whom were Sam and Tom) hopped into my vehicle. It would be a short ride into town for two of the passengers, so nobody decided to put on their seat belts except for me. One of my buddies was riding in the back of the car where cargo is supposed to be stored. No big deal though. I was taking him to the convenience store, which was close, right on the edge of the town.

I dropped two of my buddies off at the convenience store around two o'clock. We said our goodbyes to the rest of the group. When we pulled away, I noticed both Sam and Tom were sitting in the back seat while the front passenger seat was vacant. Being funny, I told them to fight over the front seat, but they decide to stay in the back. I thought to myself that their choice was weird, but whatever. I started to drive back through town as Sam had left his car at my house. Tom was going to stay at Sam's house for the night. As soon as I hit the far end of town, I stepped on the accelerator and started speeding. I was going about eighty miles per hour (mph) in a fifty-five mph speed limit area and having a good time passing cars along the highway. About a quarter mile after the last stop light in town, I made a left turn onto the dark winding road where my house is located.

I knew the road like the back of my hand, but due to my impaired state of mind, I started speeding again, reaching speeds of eighty to eighty-five mph in a forty-five mph zone. The road has a few straight-aways with a few subtle turns, but then the road drops in elevation and has a sharp left turn. The speed limit for the turn is thirty-five mph. On a good day, I could make the turn while driving fifty mph. That night I was showing off and didn't have a care in the world. I reached the corner going about seventy-five mph.

I lost control as the tires on my car started to squeal and smoke. My car *slid out* and slammed into the end of the guardrail and into a dirt embankment. The impact sent my four-wheel drive spinning and flipping at the same time. The three of us were jerked every which way like rag dolls. My seatbelt held me in place while I held onto the steering wheel with a death grip. Sam and Tom, who were sitting in the backseat weren't so fortunate. On the first of eleven flips, they were ejected from the vehicle. Sam slammed into a ravine of rocks and broke his neck, killing him instantly.

Thrown out of the window Tom landed in a patch of grass in the ravine, knocked unconscious with a few broken ribs. I held onto the steering wheel as the glass shattered and the metal twisted in havoc. The wreck took about ten seconds before I came to a rest about thirty yards down the road, over a small hill and at the base of another hill. It was 2:15 am. After coming to a stop, I took a breath and realized I was alright.

Nothing serious happened to me, but then my friends came to mind. I looked toward the back seat, but I couldn't see anything, as the moon didn't provide much light since the area was covered by the thick oak trees. I reached for my ignition keys because the key chain had a little flashlight attached to them, but they wouldn't budge. When my eyes adjusted to the darkness, I took my seatbelt off, turned around again and realized nobody was in the back seat. I realized that both of my friends had been ejected from the vehicle. All I saw was a mangled seat. My heart sank and I went into panic mode. I started screaming their names over and over again at the top of my lungs.

"Sam! Tom!, Tom! Sam!"

I was scared for my friends' lives more than anything I had experienced in my life. I continued yelling their names as I crawled out of the driver side window, slicing my arm on the broken glass, but that was the least of my worries. I scrambled to my feet and climbed up to the road. I slipped on rocks and bruised my shins along the way. Tom had finally regained consciousness and climbed up to the road to join me. I was relieved to see him, but I still called for Sam. After a few more minutes of calling for my friend, I had a bright idea.

The idea was to call his cell phone and hope its ring tone or vibration would wake him up or at least lead me to his location. When I called his phone number I saw a small light show up in the middle of the road about fifty feet away. I ran over to his phone, but Sam was nowhere near it. My heart sank. My next thought was to call my parents. They would be able to help. I never thought of calling 911 because I was so distraught.

My parents arrived within five minutes because the wreck happened a couple miles from my home. As they got out of the truck, they thought everything was fine. I told them everything and they called 911 immediately. In her pajamas, my mom decided to go back home and change into warmer clothes as it was cold outside. When she turned the truck around to head home, the headlights shone on Sam as he laid motionless on the shoulder of the road.

My dad and I ran over to Sam, picked him up off the ground and tried to wake him up. I started to cry. My dad took him and started cardiopulmonary resuscitation (CPR). It was of no use. It was clear he had already passed away. As my dad tried to give him CPR, each breath escaped through the hole in the back of his neck. I went into shock as I looked over the horrific scene: Sam in a pool of blood and gray brain matter underneath him. I could even see where he landed on the side of the hill and rolled down, disturbing the fresh tall grass along the way.

> It is illegal for adults to drive with a BAC of .08% or higher. It is illegal for anyone under age 21 to drive after drinking any alcohol in all US states.
>
> Center for Disease Control and Prevention website

As I stared into space toward the hill, the paramedics and California Highway Patrol (CHP) arrived. One paramedic came over to me and sat me down at the base of hill, while a couple others ran to Sam's side. I was told to stay still while they put a neck brace on me. When an officer came over to me all I could say was, "I killed him. I killed Sam."

I started sobbing and told the officer that I was drunk when I crashed my four-wheel drive vehicle. I kept repeating myself as they put me on a stretcher and wheeled me into the back of an ambulance. Before I was placed in the ambulance, the officer gave me a breathalyzer and I blew a 0.14 blood alcohol concentration (BAC) level, which is almost twice the legal limit for adults over twenty-one years old. I was three months shy of my eighteenth birthday, and I had only been driving by myself for three hundred and sixty days. Still on a restricted license, I had a curfew and was not allowed to have passengers.

On the way to the hospital, the CHP officer asked me all the normal questions after an auto collision. I had no injuries other than the cuts on my arm and one on my face that gave me a black eye. Not wanting to accept the fact that Sam was dead, I asked the paramedic who was scrubbing and cleaning my cuts, what had happened to him. She said she wasn't sure but it didn't look promising. I went back into shock and sobbed like a baby as they continued cleaning my cuts. I didn't say much after that.

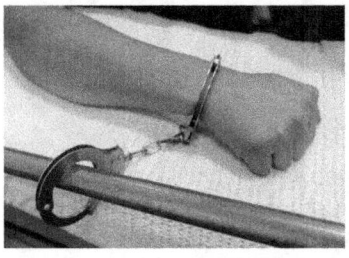

Upon arrival at the hospital, I was handcuffed to the bed. It was reality slapping me in the face. I finally drifted off to sleep and when I woke up it was time to leave. Since I was still a minor, I was released from police custody into the custody of my parents. I was terrified. I had just caused an auto collision, which took one of my friend's life and seriously injured the other.

For a couple weeks after that fatal morning, I shut myself in my bedroom away from everything. I was depressed and in denial about the wreck. I didn't want to talk to anyone, and most certainly I didn't want to face reality. No matter what, I was going to have to face the consequences of my decisions.

My dad and I went to the towing company that had pulled my vehicle out of the ravine, paid the storage fees and signed a release for the vehicle. It was the first and only time I saw my four-wheel drive vehicle after the wreck. I was surprised Tom and I were able to walk away from it. I'll never forget it. It brought back all the memories from that tragic night which I have to live with for the rest of my life. I still think about it every day.

IN HIS OWN WORDS
Darrell, Former EMT/Paramedic

As a young boy, I had an innate ability to help others in crisis. When I was a boy scout I discovered that when fellow campers hurt themselves with scraped knees, cut fingers and twisted ankles, I was the one they came running to for first aid. I was always calm in nature and blood didn't bother me. The television show *Emergency!* (1972-1979) fascinated me and because of the show, I became a paramedic.

First, I was trained as an EMT-A (Emergency Medical Technician), which meant that I was ambulance certified. Basically, an EMT is certified to assist medical personnel with basic medical treatments. My initial training started in 1988, which lead to further training and in 1990 I received

my paramedic certification. The difference between the two jobs is that the paramedic receives more advanced training. My education included: administering IVs, defibrillator and drugs per emergency room doctor direction and advanced life support. Along with more on the job training came more responsibilities, but I enjoyed the work. I was twenty-six years old when I received my paramedic patch and was certified by the state of Arkansas.

Early in my career as an EMT, I was assigned to an ambulance to work alongside a man who became my partner and mentor. One of the very first tragic emergencies that I worked as an EMT was a fatal auto collision. I remember the event vividly, even though it was thirty years ago.

It was a hot, muggy night about two o'clock in the morning. As an EMT, I was always equipped with a pager and radio ready to receive any emergency call. My partner and I were in the emergency unit talking. We were parked at a main intersection in the city that was just minutes from a major hospital. As we talked, I heard a loud bang. I knew it was a car collision, and it was close to where we were parked. My partner commented, "We're going to get that call." My partner, who was a seventeen-year veteran paramedic and had a sixth sense, knew when we would get a call.

Our pagers went off simultaneously and the dispatcher made contact with us. She told us that a MVA (Motor Vehicle Accident) just happened and gave us the location. We looked at each other and knew whatever we came upon when we arrived wasn't going to be good. I started the truck, pulled out of the parking lot and immediately saw the collision.

My partner and I were the first on the scene because we were about a block away. We immediately identified the vehicles involved in the collision, one was a small truck, the other a small compact car. The cars had spun due to the collision and were facing in opposite directions based on the impact. As the paramedic and senior person on duty, my partner assigned the car to me and then headed toward the truck. Whether the people involved in the crash are the victim(s) and/or the drunk driver, all causalities are triaged to determine who receives assistance first according to the severity of the injuries.

I quickly walked over to the car, but when I arrived it was empty. I thought to myself that the driver had been ejected and started to look around for a body. Since I couldn't find the driver, I walked back to the truck to help my partner. My first visual of the damage to the truck was on the passenger side where I saw a young girl with downs syndrome pinned and crushed inside. My partner stated that she was deceased and to help the father who was driving the truck.

I climbed into the bed of the truck and reached through the rear window, into the cab and held C-Spine immobilization (a stiff neck device to keep the neck from moving). The man was conscious and asking about his daughter. He asked that I please help her. Thinking she was alive, I tried taking her pulse on two separate occasions, but both times I tried, I could not find a pulse. She had severe body and head trauma, but I saw no blood. When people are involved in a car crash and they are deceased, there is blood, but it doesn't seep out of the body.

I was very upset that the young girl was killed in the collision. But my attention needed to be focus on the man I was helping and the other driver who we still had not located. The fire department was next to arrive on the scene and they started to cut the truck into pieces in order to remove both the father and daughter. Then the police department showed up. Once the man was extricated from his vehicle, I told a female police officer who arrived on the scene that we didn't know the location of the other driver.

The father was conscious, but in critical condition. He had multiple body fractures, lacerations and profuse bleeding. My partner and I were ready to transport the patient to the hospital that was close to the scene of the collision but were told by the dispatcher to take the man to the local university hospital because it was a Level 1 trauma center. As we were preparing to leave the scene, I overheard one of the firefighters' report to the female police officer that there was a man sitting on the sidewalk of a business down the street and that he appeared to have substantial injuries.

It turns out that that man was the driver of the car I originally went to attend. The driver tried to run away, but due to the severity of his injuries, he was unable to run very far. He had leg, arm, hand and facial injuries that were severe, and his lower jaw was hanging by a facial muscle. Literally, the lower half his face was torn off. I called dispatch to send another paramedic unit to assist this driver.

My partner and I left for the hospital. I was driving the ambulance while my partner was in the back of the unit attending to the father. As we arrived at the university hospital, the father coded (he died). We quickly moved him into the emergency room and started life support. I administered CPR (cardiopulmonary resuscitation) alongside the emergency medical staff and literally straddled the father to compress his chest. Upon finding a pulse, the patient was turned over to the emergency room staff. I returned to the truck to clean and decontaminate it.

As I was decontaminating the truck, the other unit arrived with the driver and I learned of the severity of his injuries. Not only was his face torn in half due to his head going through the car windshield, but all the bones in his fingers, hands and arms were shattered due to the tight grip of his hands on the steering wheel as he braced himself for the crash. The driver thought he had a green light, when in reality it was the truck that had a green arrow to make a left-hand turn. Going fifty five miles per hour (mph) in a forty mph zone, the drunk driver *T-boned* the father and daughter as they made a legal left turn.

Back at the crime scene, several firefighters worked fervently to free the young girl. When I asked the first responders about her, I was told that the firefighters had to cut the car completely apart in order to retrieve her body. She was dead on the scene (DOS). Protocol requires the body to be transported to the hospital where she was pronounced dead on arrival (DOA) by the medical staff. She had severe trauma. She was basically crushed in the truck due to the impact of the speeding car driven by the drunk driver.

I didn't finish my shift that early morning. Instead I drove home to my wife and two young daughters and gave them each a kiss.

Two weeks later, I was at work stocking the paramedic truck when the father and mother of the deceased daughter showed up at the headquarters. He was in a wheelchair and still battered and bruised from the collision. They thanked me and my partner for helping him and his daughter. My partner shared that their daughter died instantly and assured them that she did not suffer. I cried as the memories from two weeks earlier flooded my mind. That was one of only a few times that I received a thank you from someone I helped.

Being a paramedic was rewarding and I enjoyed helping others. I provided aid to numerous DUI collision patients and handled the injuries and deaths without incident. But after experiencing deaths of infants and small children over the years, the job finally took a toll on my state of mind. One day I called my supervisor and told him that I could no longer be a paramedic.

It has been over twenty years since I served as an EMT/Paramedic. I resigned from my career and started experiencing health issues. I was diagnosed with bi-polar disorder. It wasn't until twenty years later that I learned that I was not bi-polar but suffered from Post-Traumatic Stress Disorder (PTSD). The nightmares had taken a toll on me. I would love to be a paramedic again, but with PTSD, I don't think I could do it. I lost too many patients.

The driver of the recounted story above was convicted of involuntary manslaughter. I was sequestered for the trial, but never had to testify. The horrible things that we do to each other saddens me. That I was unable to save many lives due to DUI saddens me. Please think before you drive impaired. It's not only your life, but the life of innocent people, their families and friends that you will save.

IN HIS OWN WORDS
Charles

To all individuals who are going through their first driving under the influence (DUI) conviction and to those who have more than one DUI conviction, I say, "Please beware." You are already on your way to total destruction. You may not even know it, nor do you have a clue of the journey you have embarked upon. You may be wondering who I am and what I am writing about.

The answer to the first question is that I'm someone who cares about what could happen to you if you continue down this road of impaired driving. Through this testimonial you are about to find out why I am writing this story. I write this essay hoping that not one of you make the same mistake I did. This is serious.

For some of you, attending a DUI school is boring and you may think to yourself, "I wasn't that drunk to be here." You can think what you want, but the point is there are numerous excuses for your irresponsible behavior. That's exactly what they are, excuses. Some of you have yet to take responsibility for your selfish conduct and the serious consequences of your actions. Some of you will take your DUI experience seriously; others of you will care less. Regardless, you will complete the class just to get your driver's license back. Some of you have no intention of stopping your irresponsible behavior of drinking alcohol and driving, which makes you extremely dangerous.

Short History:

For the last twenty-four years, I was a successful Aerospace Structural Engineer. I worked for some of the major aerospace companies in the world. My thirty-four year career started in the 1970s when I was seventeen years old and enlisted in the US Air Force after graduating from high school. I had a very good life and career. I was married with three kids, had a beautiful house, and multiple cars. Every aspect of my life was wonderful, or so I thought.

I mentioned these facts because I had no excuse for my irresponsible and selfish behavior. My drinking started as a reward system. Every Friday after work, my co-workers and I would visit the local bar for drinks and talk about the prior week's events. Afterwards I would drive home. I could have asked someone to drive me home if I felt too intoxicated, but the thought of leaving my car in a parking lot wasn't happening! So, I would drive home. Sometimes I wondered how I made it home because I didn't remember anything the next day. I am sure some of you can identify with that attitude; yet, you continue the risky behavior.

After years of risky behavior, the inevitable is bound to happen. When I received my first DUI, I went through the routine. Some of you know it. That one experience should have ended any future encounters with drinking and driving. Just going to jail should have been enough. For a brief moment, it was, but, the following weekend I acted as if nothing ever happened. I thought DUI school was a joke.

Do you really think I stopped driving just because I didn't have my driver's license? I had other things to do. I became so arrogant that I never gave any serious thought to my behavior or that I was putting people's lives at risk. The tragic part about my thought process and behavior was that my wife and kids would ask me all the time to stop my drinking and driving. Did I stop because of my arrogance? NO! I would tell myself, "I know what I am doing. I have this under complete control."

I had many excuses for not doing what was right and proper. I continued to make excuses for my drinking. I completely missed the whole point. It's just not my drinking, it's my driving! These two actions do not complement one another. They do not mix with each other; yet I continued these two actions. For me, drinking and driving became a usual occurrence. It began to escalate. I was arrested a couple more times for DUI. Finally, the courts felt I needed to spend some time in jail, so I was sentenced to thirty days here, sixty days there, and so on. I never served the entire time anyway, so it didn't really affect me too much.

I still had my job, family, home, and car. Now, for most reasonably thinking people, coming through all that mess, at some point one would check his/herself and stop the irresponsible behavior. In my distorted thinking, I didn't see anything wrong nor did I see the dangerous journey on which I had embarked. For approximately fifteen years, I acted indulgently. In 2005, a friend invited me to a barbecue. I wasn't doing anything that day, except relaxing at home so I decided to go. My whole motive for attending was to enjoy the evening and eat some good barbecue, nothing else. Drinking was not on my mind.

As a matter of fact, there wasn't any alcohol at the gathering when I arrived, but as the evening progressed an individual showed up with several bottles of alcohol. Then, several people started to drink as the party got underway. I thought, "Well one drink won't hurt." Sound familiar? Add to the fact that I was only a fifteen-minute drive from my house, "What could possibly happen in that short time frame?" So, I decided to have one drink, which turned into two, three, and by the time the fourth drink came around it was almost two o'clock in the morning. My wife had been calling me all evening to come home, but in my arrogance, I didn't take heed and dismissed her plea to come home. Bad, bad mistake. That was a decision I would regret for the rest of my life.

I never made it home. I thought I could drive home, but I was so impaired that all I remember was entering onto the freeway; thereafter, everything was a blank. I had blacked out. Somehow, I made a U-turn in the middle of the freeway and was driving in the opposite direction into on-coming traffic. When I regained some consciousness, all that I noticed were the red and blue lights flashing all around me.

I realized that I was in an auto collision, but I didn't know how bad. I remember a highway patrol officer asking me some questions, but I don't remember his exact questions. I slightly remember being driven to the hospital due to my injuries. The major injury I sustained was a fractured pelvis in six different places (which I still suffer from). It was not until I was in the recovery room that I finally found out the tragic, horrific devastation I caused. I had a head-on collision with three teenagers; two fatalities and one seriously injured. When I first heard the news I truly thought I was either dreaming or they were speaking of some other collision, because I thought that there was no way on this God given earth that I had killed someone, let alone two people. I could not fathom this reality in a million years. God would not allow that to happen. But no matter how much I wished it wasn't true, reality set in. It was all too real. Two young men, seventeen and eighteen years old, lost their lives because of my arrogance and selfish behavior. Now what?

In the state of California, drinking and driving with fatalities takes on a whole new meaning than most states. If you drink and drive and cause a fatality without any prior DUI, you will most likely receive a vehicular manslaughter conviction. But, if you have a prior DUI conviction, it is a different story.

When you are arrested and convicted for DUI, two of the conditions for probation are to complete a certified DUI school and to sign a Tahl Waiver, which states, "If you are arrested for any DUI where there are fatalities you can be charged with murder."

Some of you remember, some don't. It does not matter because you have already been convicted of a DUI. Remember in the beginning I told you to beware. If you have been convicted of at least one DUI, if you are arrested ever again and there are fatalities, you will be charged with Gross Vehicular Manslaughter while intoxicated. This carries a fifteen year to life sentence due to your prior DUI conviction.

Furthermore, you can be charged with Second Degree Murder, which also carries a fifteen year to life term. Why? There are several reasons why. First, it's called *Implied Malice* (California Penal Code 188) which states,

Malice may be implied when a person, knowing that his conduct endangers the life of another, nonetheless acts deliberately, with conscious disregard for life.

In very simple terms it means, "You have a knowing knowledge that drinking and driving are dangerous." How does the court know? First, you attended DUI School. Second, there is a California State Supreme Court case called *People V. Watson* (30 CAL.3d 290, 637 P.2d 279, 179 Cal. Rptr. 43).

Prosecutors can use this as a legal precedent to charge individuals with a DUI prior conviction with DUI Second Degree Murder.

Now, you think this only happens in California. Yes, California has strong case law precedence, but all states have seriously cracked down on fatal DUI auto collisions. If you have a fatality and a DUI conviction, you are likely to receive a life sentence. It's basically the same nationwide. In the end, I received thirty-eight years to life.

My life as I knew it was completely over; everything is gone. Wife, children, friends, home, job, car and career, Gone! Liberty, gone! All because of selfishness, ego, arrogance and irresponsible behavior. This horrific collision could have been avoided if I had listened to people's warnings and thought about my behavior. Some of you probably believe that this situation will never happen to you. Trust me; that is foolish and idiotic thinking. If you continue down the road of drinking and driving or whatever you do that impairs your driving; the odds are not in your favor.

When you kill someone, that person's life, his/her family's lives, and your life will never be the same. It's not a situation or circumstance that you can ever pay for, fix or make right. Please, think about that for a minute! Don't sacrifice the lives of others because of your irresponsible behavior of driving under the influence. You have no right to do that.

Please don't make the same mistakes I did. The cost is too high (the death of someone, your death, or life in prison). Right now, you have the opportunity of a wholesome life. You have a choice. Do not allow your ego or whatever motivates you to continue driving under the influence. You will regret it for the rest of your life, your family's and other's lives!

I know this plea may not affect everyone, but I hope it will affect some while giving others something to think about.

IN HIS OWN WORDS
Leroy

I have been clean and sober for thirty years, and it is a wonderful feeling. I started drinking at the age of sixteen. I did not drink every day but when I did, it was quite heavily. I drank so much that I would blackout and only remember bits and pieces of my drunken stupor. I had no regards for the law, others or myself. I had no idea of the number of crimes I had committed while being drunk. I heard from other people about my behavior, and afterwards, I would feel so ashamed and embarrassed. I would become angry and violent, just making a fool of myself.

I never tried to make amends for my actions. I would sweep the consequences under the rug and let time fix them. At times, I would get in my vehicle and drive for hours with no idea where I was driving. Each time I drove drunk, I was putting the lives of others and my life in danger. I was not concerned about anyone else as long as I wasn't pulled over by the police or got into a collision.

On one occasion, I stayed up all night drinking and doing drugs with my brother and a few friends and lost all track of time. I realized I had to be to work in less than two hours. I could not sober up in that short amount of time, so I went to work drunk. The next day I learned that I had said something to hurt one of my female co-worker's feelings. I knew then (and now) it was due to my alcohol use. I felt like a damn fool but did nothing to make amends to her or any of my other co-workers. Again, I let time fix the consequences of my actions.

On another occasion, when my brother and I arrived home

California Office of Traffic Safety

drunk, we didn't know that my mom and dad had company. It was the first time the company had ever been to our house. What an embarrassment it was for everyone as we staggered in the front door. What a good first impression we made!

Another time, I picked up my girlfriend, so she could celebrate my twenty-first birthday with my family and me. We had a few beers before going to my party. She wanted a pack of cigarettes, and even though I did not approve of her smoking, I bought them for her anyway. When I returned to my car she was not there. All sorts of horrible thoughts went through my mind and I began to panic.

I did not know what I was going to tell her family, my family or the police. I somehow felt they would all blame me. A few minutes later, I saw her walking toward my car. She bummed a cigarette from a total stranger as she could not wait for me to come out of the store. I completely lost control. I pushed her to the ground and cussed her out, then told her that she ruined my birthday party. I told her to get in my car as I was taking her home and did not want to see her anymore. I was in such a hurry to take her home that I was driving recklessly. I was speeding and ran a red light on purpose causing us to be in a car collision.

My girlfriend was seriously hurt. Her face hit the windshield and there was blood all over her. She was taken by ambulance to the hospital and had several stitches. Afterwards, my dad drove both of us to her house. It was embarrassing for me when she walked through the front door. I blamed the collision on the other driver to avoid punishment and criticism. I never made amends to my girlfriend. She called off our relationship. Had I been sober, I never would have behaved in such a manner.

I am so ashamed and embarrassed. I made a fool of myself, and it brings me to tears as I look back at my past behavior of drinking. I never made amends to any of the people I harmed. I never took responsibility for my actions. I drank to have fun and to fit in with my friends. I clearly had no regard for the law, others, or myself.

I enabled others to drink, especially those who were underage. Alcohol did nothing but cause others and me problems. I wonder how many people I influenced who became an alcoholic. I urge all young guys and girls to think about the seriousness of drinking and the consequences that come with it. If you do have a drinking problem, do not be ashamed or embarrassed to ask for help. That is the first step in making amends.

I have been attending A.A. (for the alcoholic) for three years and Al-Anon (for family members of an alcoholic) meetings over four years. I now have a better understanding of the problem alcohol causes; not only for the alcoholic, but for others around him or her. The way I feel about alcohol today, I will do whatever I can to stay clean and sober the rest of my life. God bless all of you.

IN HIS OWN WORDS
Conrado

My name is Conrado and I'm forty-two years old. I would like to share my testimony about my alcoholism and the crime I committed while under the influence of alcohol. I grew up with my parents, two sisters and a brother. I come from an alcoholic family, on both sides. Growing up I remember watching my family and other people getting drunk on every occasion or special event. I came to believe that drinking alcohol was a normal activity for adults. Throughout my childhood and adolescence, I also witnessed a lot of domestic violence. I eventually became a very timid, fearful and angry youth with low self-esteem. I was an insecure person. I didn't receive the appreciation, approval, recognition or guidance that I needed from my father.

At fifteen years old, I started drinking alcohol to escape the reality of the life I was living. My first drunken episode was at the age of sixteen, when I started hanging out with older guys with whom I found acceptance and gratification. The alcohol felt good because I found a way to ease the pain I was feeling. When intoxicated I discovered that I had confidence to socialize with other people, especially females who I wasn't able to approach when sober. I made alcohol and drinking my friend because it was a cool thing to do and I felt that I could do anything. Within time, my drinking increased from occasionally to a daily basis. At that time, I didn't acknowledge any of my problems, so I continued drinking to the point of passing out and having major blackouts.

In 2003, I was arrested for my first driving under the influence (DUI). I went to jail for a couple hours only to be booked and released. Months later I returned to court to be convicted and ordered to pay court fines. This was the first time I was arrested, and I didn't take it seriously. It wasn't a big deal to me. It was like giving me a slap on the hand. I thought, "I won't do it again; it was just a day of bad luck." Although the judge ordered me to attend Alcoholics Anonymous (A.A.) meetings, a MADD (Mothers Against Drunk Drivers) panel, and to do community service, I didn't learn that I had an alcohol problem or that I had to change my life.

I didn't take A.A. seriously, I thought it wasn't for me. I continued my alcoholic life, drinking daily. I was in total denial about my alcoholism. What made it worse was that I thought I was able to drink and drive. I felt entitled to drive. I believed that I was a better driver and was not hurting anybody. I told myself, "Drinking and driving isn't a crime." I was a hard-working man who deserved to have a drink to relax after work. No one could tell me otherwise.

In 2005, I was arrested for a second DUI. Again, I went through the process: more A.A. meetings, more DUI classes, and another MADD panel where my fines increased to thousands of dollars. I ended up serving sixty days in the county jail on weekends. This enabled me to work during the week. I still didn't get it. I continued drinking. I even turned myself in drunk; how insane was that? I was placed on probation for three years and had my license suspended for a year, but I still continued my routine as if nothing had happened.

My family didn't know about my previous arrests, so I acted normal in front of them. I continued drinking and partying at every celebration, but most of the time I drank in my house alone. I didn't want to stop drinking because I thought I couldn't function without alcohol. I drove hundreds of times drunk, believing I would never be caught drinking and driving again.

Watching videos of the people killed by drunk drivers at a MADD panel was very emotional for me. The mothers talked about their loved ones who were murdered by drunk drivers and their own pain. They suffer with the tragic reality that they will be without their loved ones for the rest of their lives. The mothers asked us to stop drinking and driving in order to prevent the killing of more innocent people. After hearing their stories, I thought about stopping my drinking, but I never sobered up. I always thought I was a better drinker and better driver than anybody else. However, I made a promise not to drink and drive again, I made that promise in my head, but I never put it into practice.

In June 2007, I made the poor decision to drink and drive

again. Once again, I thought nothing would happen to me and that I was okay to drive because I was only *buzzed,* not drunk. Sadly, I collided into the back of another car on the freeway at a speed of seventy-five miles per hour (mph) in a sixty-five mph zone. The impact was greater because the other car was driving fifty-five mph due to mechanical problems. Unlike my previous DUIs, this time I didn't make it home. Because of my selfishness and unwillingness to change, I murdered a woman, one of the two passengers in the other car. I was convicted of Second Degree Murder in 2009.

Later, I learned that she was fifty years old and passed away ten days after the collision. She was a wife, a mother, a daughter, sister, aunt, a member of her church, and a friend. She was everything to her family. I murdered an innocent person because I couldn't deal with my issues and emotions in a proper way. I murdered her because I was a totally irresponsible person.

She was murdered because I am an alcoholic. Now I understand that I was a monster behind the wheel, putting many people in danger. At that time, I didn't care about myself. I didn't care about my life, so I didn't think about the safety of others. I was a very selfish person. I put alcohol before everything else.

I'm serving a fifteen year to life sentence for the crime I committed. I'm in my tenth year, and there is not a single day when I wake up that I don't think about what I have done. Waking up every day in a prison cell furnished with a bunk, a locker, a toilet and a *celly* is not always pleasant. But, the possibility that I might die in prison doesn't depress my spirit or bring me down, because I have the potential to be a better human being. I refuse to give up.

Instead, I made the decision to educate myself. I take A.A. seriously and work the steps. Today I am a sober person. I don't rely on alcohol to *function* when dealing with my emotions. I face my issues the proper way. I ask for help by talking to my sponsor, psychologist or a friend. I use the A.A. tools and coping skills to continue my sobriety. I am and always will be an alcoholic, but today I'm a new person. I'm responsible, mature, humble, compassionate and a believer in God as I understand Him.

I'm facing a harsh sentence, but it is nothing compared to the lives of the woman's family who have to live without her. A.A. taught me how to apply the spiritual principles in my daily living, and I now have an understanding of the impact of my crime. The physical, emotional, economical, mental and spiritual harm that I caused to the victim's immediate family, her in-laws and friends. This also includes the community as a whole: witnesses, California Highway Patrol officers, doctors, nurses, judges, jurors and my family. All of them were affected by my selfish, evil decisions.

I know the day I arrived in prison, but I don't know when I will be released. Drinking and driving is a serious crime. I encourage everybody reading this essay to think about your behavior and change your life around. Make a positive decision. Avoid the risk of killing another innocent person rather than having to spend the rest of your life behind concrete walls. Use common sense. Think about your safety and the safety of others. Responsible people don't behave like I did. Responsible people don't drink and drive while impaired.

IN HER OWN WORDS
Rae Ellen, DUI Fatal Collision Crash Survivor

Rae Ellen Foy was the sole survivor of a fatal collision caused by a drunk driver. She lost her husband and three young children that day and spent the next four weeks in the hospital due to the severity of her injuries. Over thirty years ago, she wrote her story in a national women's magazine and shared about the initial weeks after the collision – the disbelief that her family was dead and about the journey of her physical recovery. Now, over forty years later Rae Ellen graciously shares about her life since the fatal auto collision. Although she states, "Sometimes my feelings are too strong to write," below is her story:

People read my story in the local newspaper and wanted to help. After my release from the hospital, I lived with my parents. Having a broken right femur, I was unable walk well and using crutches was difficult due to my broken left arm. Also, my left cornea was slashed in the collision, so my vision was impaired. It was rough. I went to doctors, took medicine and did physical therapy. The physical healing was slow, but friends and family supplied all the love and help I needed to keep going.

The pain and trauma of the emotional upset of losing my husband, our five-year old twin girls and twenty-month old baby girl hindered the healing of my physical injuries. I felt my life was over. They were my life and they were gone. I had no desire to get better for me. I wanted my husband and girls!

In order to begin the emotional healing process, I had to accept the loving help from friends and family. This meant I had to hide all the envy I felt. They still had their families and I did not. I would tell them, "Never forget how much your family loves and appreciates you." My pastor and well-meaning friends listened when I talked to them.

It took many steps to get back to real life again. Once

physically healed, I left my parents' house and returned to my home. When I was well enough I returned to my former part-time job as a secretary in a small office.

A few months after the fatal collision, I read a magazine article about a new organization, MADD - Mothers Against Drunk Driving. There was no local chapter where I lived, so I contacted MADD and asked how to start one in my area. With the help from leaders of other chapters, we began a local chapter of MADD. There was a need for the chapter and it gave me a focus and a purpose.

Many victims came forward. It allowed me to talk with other victims as I knew I wasn't alone in my recovery. We all had been deeply hurt and it would take a lot of sharing to begin the healing process. Everyone shared their pain and that helped all of us to heal.

It reached a point when drunk drivers were court ordered to attend the MADD meetings in order for them to hear the victims' stories. They cried with us and some attendees came to an understanding of the damage they caused from their drinking and driving. Many of these people came up to apologize to me and the other victims after we shared our stories. They realized that they could become victims at some point as well, if their drunk driving wasn't brought under control. That was important to all of us who shared our loved ones stories.

My life has changed a lot over the years. I married a man who was a widower with four children almost forty years ago. I was able to get pregnant and had a son, who is now thirty-eight years old, married and has a son and daughter of his own. My husband and I have thirteen grandchildren from my husband's four children and two more from the son we share. We enjoy fifteen grandchildren! That's a real bonus after losing my family.

I never met the man who caused the car crash that killed my family. But, I do know he is dead now. What happened was God's will, so I have had to accept it and forgive him. Sometimes it is difficult to accept God's will, but we have to do it. I know my first husband and our three daughters are in Heaven, and I pray I am able to join them someday. Until then, they are always in my heart, thoughts and prayers.

August 7, 2018 was forty-four years after the fatal car crash that took my family. Many friends and family still miss my husband, Duane, and our daughters, Lori, Lisa and Traci. Would my twins still look alike if they were alive? I was never able to see my daughters go to school, graduate high school or go to college. I never experienced their falling in love, getting married or having babies of their own. I love them and miss them every day. My husband and I didn't get to live our lives together and celebrate what would be our fiftieth wedding anniversary. All because of a drunk driver. Who knows if one of our daughters would have become president or done something phenomenal for the world? A drunk driver took these answers away from me.

For every person who dies from a drunk driver, the whole world suffers because we don't know what this person would have contributed to our universe. That means not just his/her mom and dad, sons and daughters, and other family and friends will suffer the loss. We all do! And why? Because someone wanted to drink and drive.

We need to make people realize why it is wrong to drink and drive. Yes, it is against the law, but there are more reasons. It takes lives! It ruins lives and it causes so much pain. It is wrong! We must stop drinking and driving!

I would like the reader to know that even though I have since remarried and given birth to another child, it doesn't take away the loss.

To other victims' families: I hope you will receive from all your friends and family the love they have for you. Love heals. You will always have your memories of your loved one(s) and will see them in Heaven someday.

To those who drink and drive: Think of the possible harm you may cause others. Do you want to harm or kill someone by driving drunk? Do you want to kill someone's child? Wife? Husband? **Think first.** A drink is never worth the price of dying. If you have been drinking, call a cab, a friend or stay where you are. **Do not drive.**

We have to put a stop to Drunk Driving!

IN HER OWN WORDS
Kellie

    I grew up in a beautiful suburban town. I had everything I ever needed and much of what I wanted too. I was a regular kid living life and trying to fit in and be a part of the crowd. I had so many friends and was thought of as one of the popular girls. Instead of feeling accepted for who I was as a person, I was insecure and felt different from my friends. I drank for the first time to fit in with the crowd. I remember vividly when I drank alcohol for the first time. It made me feel alive. No more insecurities, and I no longer cared what people thought about me. I blacked out the first night I drank alcohol, so I thought it was a normal part of drinking. I learned later that it's a major warning sign of alcoholism.

    I was in the seventh grade when I first drank alcohol and chased that false sense of liquid courage with a vengeance. All I wanted was to know where the next party was being held. I soon became the party girl who was influencing others around me. My decisions of choosing alcohol over responsibilities came quick. I started slacking in sports, school, ambition and family life. I only lived for the next party.

    This lifestyle followed me throughout high school. As much as I thought I was having fun, this *fun* had its consequences. I was kicked out of summer school, dances and skipped school because of alcohol. I embarrassed myself at parties. I made poor decisions in my choice of friends and snuck out of the house to go to parties. At the time, my poor decisions were worth any consequence I received.

    I let my classmates down on a final group project for English. I was to be the main character in a play. The night before I chose to go to a club and instead of waking up by my alarm clock, I woke up to my phone ringing with the person on the other end asking why I wasn't in class. I let my classmates down when I arrived at school still drunk from the night before and recited my role without enthusiasm. I was too hungover to care.

I was voted the person *Always Partying* in my high school senior yearbook. I was proud of that designation. My yearbook quote also stated, "I live for the night that I'll never remember with the friends I'll never forget." All I wanted to do was party.

Every problem in my life had the common denominator of alcohol but I didn't want to accept it. I had every excuse, "I was having fun." "I was young, my behavior was normal." "I couldn't be an alcoholic."

Based on my past behaviors, when I drank alcohol I never knew what was going to happen that night or morning. My temperament could be happy, angry, crying, or belligerent. I could make a huge scene. One night I went to a club with a so-called friend of mine and planned to sleep at her house. I always got insanely drunk and knew I would not be able to drive. I ended up blacking out even before we went into the club, but continued to drink. We ended up being kicked out of the club because I could not stand up straight.

I don't remember anything from that night. Alcohol lowers judgement significantly, so I'm not sure if I said I was okay to drive home or maybe I was so obnoxious my friends wanted me to go home. Either way, I ended up driving that night in a blackout. I traveled two hours heading north thinking I was driving home, but I was so insanely drunk that I was lost. I remember a glimpse of a county sign and thought to myself, "Why am I here?" Police records show I made a U-Turn on the freeway and proceeded to drive south in the north bound lanes. I collided head-on with another vehicle that had four young girls in it. I thank God every day that not one of them was not killed, but they were severely injured. I severely injured myself as well. I would never in a million years intentionally hurt anyone, but alcohol leads to very poor decision-making and hurting innocent people.

I wish I could say it was a wake-up call, but it wasn't. I was in total denial. I thought the collision was an accident. I was young and naïve. I used every excuse in the book to look at myself and see how alcohol was affecting my life. I thought alcoholism was for older men, the homeless, bikers, etc. I didn't believe I could be one. My biggest excuse was I was just young and having fun. I surrounded myself with people who drank just like me; therefore, I thought everything I was doing was normal.

I have learned throughout the years that if nothing changes, *nothing changes.* I found myself doing some insane things. The definition of insanity is doing the same thing repeatedly expecting a different result. I tried to control my drinking, but it never worked. I tried changing my environment. I tried anything I could think of to control my alcohol consumption, but I continued to drink until I blacked out. My drinking alcohol led to making poor choices.

I felt horrible for the pain and suffering I had caused the people who were affected by my actions when I drank – my family, my friends, my classmates, my co-workers, and the girls I crashed into – yet, I continued to party. It was the only way I knew how to have fun. My drinking caused so much wreckage, but I downplayed the consequences. I failed in college, ruined relationships, hurt the people I loved and cared about, and was almost sentenced to prison.

When my case went to trial every person who testified against me in court wanted me incarcerated. The judge decided to give me a second chance and sentenced me with a felony drunk driving charge and an

eight year joint suspended sentence with the stipulation that I would successfully finish probation, not drink alcohol, and have my driver's license suspended for three years. In addition, I spent five months in county jail as part of my sentence. In my cell, I found a book published by Alcoholics Anonymous (A.A.) and started reading it. As I read the book, I found myself relating to the content about alcoholism.

I swore I would never drink alcohol and drive again. I made that promise to myself. Unfortunately, within two months after my wrong way driving collision, I started drinking again. Finally, I had my wake-up call. After a night of partying, I went to bed and slept about seven hours. In the morning, I woke up and thought I was just tired. The reality was that I was hungover. I proceeded to get into my car and drive home but was immediately pulled over by a law enforcement officer for speeding. The officer asked me if I had been drinking. I was offended. Of course, I had not been drinking! It was 11 am and I did not drive impaired anymore. I was still on felony probation for the DUI that I had received in 2007. I was given a sobriety test and I blew a 0.21 blood alcohol concentration (BAC) level. I failed. I was arrested for my second driving under the influence (DUI).

The consequence of my poor decisions – first, to drink alcohol while on probation and then to drive hungover – lead to my sentence of up to eight years in prison to be administered. I was twenty-one years old. I no longer had liquid courage to comfort me and was faced with the ugliness of my decisions. My life in prison was the scariest thing that I ever had to experience. It was the biggest adjustment in my life, and I didn't know how I was going to handle it. I had to adapt to a lifestyle that I never experienced before. Removed from all the people I had known and loved, I now had to adapt to my new surroundings. I was not allowed to use the prison phone for more than four months upon entering prison. I learned quickly that I could not trust other convicts. I never felt so hopeless in my life, but I had to adjust quickly because I really had no other choice for the next seven years.

The first few years in prison were rough. I tried my best to get by and keep a low profile. I felt like I didn't fit in and was so lonely. My family came to visit me when they could, but to be stripped of my freedom and rights was torture. I had to do whatever I was told – when and where to eat, when to work in the kitchen, when to shower, to name a few of the instructions I had to follow. Basically, all my daily activities were determined for me. I was bullied and put down daily by other female inmates. Soon, I realized that something had to change because I did not want to live like I was living anymore.

I learned that it was important to be of service to others and stop thinking about myself. I joined A.A. in prison and found there were women who wanted to better themselves just like I wanted. Life started to change as I changed my thought process and behaviors. I no longer wanted to be identified as the party girl. I took advantage of self-help groups that the prison offered and attended an independent college. Wanting to help others, I became an inmate firefighter and served more than four years in Malibu's conservation camp. I worked as a crew leader for the fire crew and did whatever I could to make the best of a horrible situation.

Now, I started making good decisions and felt comfortable

in my own skin. I was released from prison a little over four years ago. The hopelessness I once felt no longer exists. My life is full of hope, and I am finally free from alcohol. Thanks to A.A., I have the tools needed to help me navigate through life. Moreover, my life now is beyond my wildest dreams. I volunteer at a local DUI school several times a month in order to bring awareness regarding the consequences of impaired driving. I have a career I love. I got married and have a new baby. All these things are gifts of sobriety, and they keep coming because I continue to make good decisions.

I never thought DUIs, auto collisions or prison would happen to me. I was a happy normal girl but when alcohol was in my system, I became someone else. Today I live a happy and joyous life. Free from my addiction, I am forever grateful. My goal is to help others with my story, so no one has to go through the pain I experienced. If alcohol seems like a natural part of your life, I can assure you it does not have to be. You too can be free from all the bad things that happened with alcohol abuse.

I love waking up without a hungover. I love knowing where my phone is located. I love knowing where I took off my shoes. I love waking up in my own bed in my pajamas knowing that I did not hurt anyone. My life is so full of hope today. What I once considered my biggest liabilities (my low self-esteem, alcoholism and prison) are now my biggest assets as they have molded me into the woman I am today.

IN HIS OWN WORDS
Jonathan G.

My name is Jonathan and I am currently sentenced to fifteen years to life for Second Degree Murder for driving under the influence (DUI) and killing two close friends of mine. Today I am reaching out and telling you my story in hopes of touching someone and preventing more deaths caused by the irresponsible crime of drinking and driving.

In 2014, a tragedy occurred for such careless behavior and two lives were taken, José and Mary. I had known José almost my entire life. We met in elementary school in the fifth grade. He had always been a great guy – funny, friendly, and energetic. Everybody enjoyed having him around all the time. Mary was a beautiful girl who was enthusiastic and very friendly. I had known Mary for about two years. We met through mutual friends. We had a great relationship, but we all had two big problems – alcohol and partying. It was a huge addiction. We never missed a weekend without drinking, smoking marijuana, popping pills, and snorting drugs. It was a huge part of our teens. Not thinking or caring what the consequences of alcohol and partying would cause, they lead us on a path of destruction. I struggled with drug addiction all my life. It began in sixth grade with smoking marijuana, which lead to drinking alcohol. By the time I entered high school, I was experimenting with other drugs such as pills, cocaine and meth.

2014 has haunted me with flashbacks and horrible nightmares for the past two years now. I remember how the night began.

Arizona Department of Transportation

My girlfriend at the time who is now my wife, left on an out-of-town family trip to the beach. I took it as an opportunity to go out for the weekend and have some fun without having to worry about my girlfriend. I began by scrolling through my contact list, calling and texting everyone I knew who were also party goers, alcoholics and drug addicts. I received a few answers back about a couple parties and met up with a good friend of mine, Tony. I have known Tony since elementary school.

About six o'clock in the evening, I took a shower, dressed and headed to the local grocery store. I bought a bottle of gin along with a gallon of orange juice, as that was my favorite alcohol combination. Upon my return from the store, my friend Sofia, who is a very close friend of Mary, came over to my house with her friends. We began drinking before we headed out to party. We started to drink and smoke. I took a prescription drug. By ten o'clock that night, one of my closest friends at the time, Mike, picked us up in his car and we headed to a party. We all got in the car. We arrived at the party and it was filled with lots of beautiful girls, drinks, and loud music. Another friend of mine, John, was the DJ. The night went on and the party ended close to two o'clock in the morning.

I told a couple of friends to meet at my house where we kept drinking and hanging out until the sun came up. This was a normal situation for us on the weekends. We got back in Mike's car and started to drive. We dropped off one of the girls who was with us, and now only two guys and two girls are in the car. By this time, we were all drunk and hyped up with the loud music. I'm hanging out of the car sun roof yelling while Mike is speeding. Mike was really into street racing and drove fast. We got back to my house and waited inside until the rest of our friends arrived. Tony, José and a couple of other friends showed up. We were outside of the house; music bumping, drinking and smoking. It's late in the morning and a couple people left. Mary asked me for a ride home because she had to get up early for work the next day. No one else had a vehicle, so I told her, "Yeah, I'll give you a ride."

Mary, José, Sofia and I got in my car. I remember as we drove, that I made a turn and headed toward the city. As a sober person I am calm and collected, but under the influence I am the complete opposite. I began speeding and showing off to look cool in front of my friends. Eventually, I blacked out and crashed into a light post going one hundred miles per hour (mph). My car split in half. I woke up in the hospital unable to feel my legs or move my body. I had a broken hip and was surrounded by police officers. My first reaction, "What happened? What is going on?"

I was scared out of my mind as the police wouldn't tell me what happened until I saw it on the news for myself. That's my story of how I killed my two friends while ruining my life. By the blessing of God, Mary survived. She walked away from the collision without any injuries and called the police and ambulance for help. It was the beginning of my journey of being locked away from my family and friends.

I wrote my story hoping to reach out and save somebody's life by making someone think twice before getting behind the wheel of a vehicle while impaired. I was always hard headed and thought that I was untouchable, and that nothing would ever happen to me. Please think before you act because one act of careless behavior, one poor choice can forever change your life in the blink of an eye.

Thank you for allowing me the chance to tell my story. Hopefully, it will reach somebody and save his/her life before he/she makes a poor choice. A decision that could drive him/her down a dark path, one that could possibly lead to his/her death, the death of somebody else, or a life sentence.

IN HIS OWN WORDS
Raymond

    In our society, getting drunk and blacking out is the cool thing to do. Musicians sing about their drunken tactics. Movies reveal to the audiences the comedic unremembered night of a drunken adventure. However, these songs and movies rarely portray the many dangers of blacking out; dangers such as sexual assault, or worse, the taking of a life. We are told to drink responsibly, but how do you responsibly poison yourself? One night I had a lot of alcohol to drink. I don't even know if I was having a good time. I blacked out. When I came to and sobered up, I realized that I was handcuffed to a table.

    A detective walked in and told me that I had crashed into a young woman. I couldn't believe it. He told me that she was in bad shape and that she might not live. That young woman did not pull through. She lost her life because of my arrogant and reckless decisions to drink alcohol and drive. I'm now in prison serving a twenty year to life sentence for Gross Vehicular Manslaughter (GVM).

    I grew up playing sports and was taught to treat others as I would like to be treated. I didn't join a gang or live a life of crime. My passion was my comic book collection. I signed up to serve in the US Army. Military service took me to Europe and Iraq; I served honorably. I continued my education and earned two Associate's and a Bachelor degree. My service to our country continued in the form of community service and employment with the US House of Representatives. I wanted to help make the world a better place; be part of the solution, not the problem.

    Now, still to this day, I cannot look in a mirror or see my reflection without feeling shame for what I have done. I remember the first time I received a visit from my wife and mother. I couldn't look them in the eye; I couldn't even look at their faces. I just sat there with my head hanging in shame and disgrace. Feeling like scum, I just sat there and sobbed.

Our society does not realize that the impact of drunk driving is similar to a weapon of mass destruction. The affects are numerous, lives are forever ruined. I took a young woman's life. I took a daughter from her parents, a sister from her siblings and a friend from her friends. I took advantage of my community's trust and I failed. I should've held myself to higher standards. The hurt and pain doesn't just stop there. In the wake of my recklessness, I also managed to hurt my family and friends. I became the epicenter of a life-time of loss, hurt, and grief by drunk driving.

Society has become culturally conditioned to believe that drinking can be responsibly executed or that it is acceptable to drink the night away as long as you have a designated driver. We are slammed with alcohol advertisements. Our television programs entertain us with shows that take place at bars or clubs. The music we listen to harmonize about alcohol fueled escapades. Nowhere are we being informed or notified of the health risks. Alcohol abuse has led to unintentional injuries, unplanned pregnancies, cancers, liver disease, digestive problems, and a host of mental health disorders.

> "More than 80 percent of movies contain depictions of alcohol use," says Dartmouth University pediatrician James D. Sargent, who has been combing films for their depictions of violence, tobacco, drugs and drinking for more than 20 years.
>
> Ben Panko, smithsonian.com, May 9, 2017

I thought I was having fun partying, but all I was doing was poisoning myself, gambling with my health and the safety of others. Drunk driving is a serious problem in our country. In 2016, the Veteran suicide rate was twenty-two a day; deaths from driving under the influence were twenty-eight a day. Drunk driving is an epidemic. There is something more going on than making the bad decisions to drink and then to drive. The issues are within the fabrics of our society. We as people have become complacent with alcohol abuse as long as no one gets hurt. Our laws seek to punish rather than prevent and treat.

Looking back, if I had known then what I know now, I would have lived a healthier life and made better choices about using alcohol. Now, I sit in a cell not knowing when I will be allowed to go home. I think about the young woman whose life I took and her family and friends whom I also have hurt.

    I think about the pain I've caused my family and friends and the devastation I've imposed on my community. No one must suffer from drunk driving's horrific impact. Learn from my story and don't drive drunk.

IN HER OWN WORDS
Deborah, Uber/Lyft Driver

UBER/LYFT HISTORY

Back when Garrett Camp and Travis Kalanick started Uber and Logan Green and John Zimmer started Lyft, an amazing concept was born. These entrepreneurs created an app for their services that allowed customers to request a driver through their smartphones. Since the birth of these two companies in 2009 (Uber) and 2010 (Lyft), the idea of ride-sharing has spread like wildfire in thousands of cities across the US. and dozens of countries.

I drive for both Uber and Lyft. You may have heard about these companies and probably have some strong opinions about either or both of them. However, Uber and Lyft have earned an impeccable reputation amongst its users. Nothing is perfect but for the most part, users of the service love it.

For the past few years, Uber had been testing a driverless car in four major US. cities including Tempe, Phoenix, Pittsburgh, and San Francisco, as well as Toronto, Canada. At the same time, Uber started discussions with legislators and authorities in those cities about the next steps for its driverless car program. However, after a fatal crash involving a pedestrian in Tempe, Arizona, which was one of its autonomous driver test sites, the ride-sharing company halted its driverless vehicle test operations in all cities.

Uber and Lyft face many obstacles as they both attempt to provide a low-cost alternative to those who do not want to use a taxicab or cannot afford the cost of transportation that it takes to use a cab. Taxicabs can be expensive and impersonal for many riders. Uber/Lyft riders know and understand that the Uber/Lyft driver has more of an investment than a *cabi*. The Uber/Lyft rider has more of a personable interest in riding in an Uber/Lyft car because the Uber/Lyft driver is offering a ride in his/her own personal vehicle. Therefore, it is a more private and personal experience for the rider.

Both Uber and Lyft have similarities. First, both companies allow a person to request a ride from their cell phone. Next, customer-marketing strategies seem quite similar. When Lyft introduces a new driver promotion, Uber does the same. When Lyft offers new users' huge amounts of free ride credit, Uber also gives their riders' account credit. When Uber invested in autonomous cars, Lyft struck a record deal with General Motors. The difference between the companies is that Uber has upscale options for people who want something more luxurious and spacious. As the bigger company, Uber is also available in many more states and countries than Lyft.

Although both companies share a wide range of customers, both compete heavily in the area of pricing. For instance, Uber adds a surge rate multiplier, which may change based on location, and can surge up to 1.3 or 2.1 times the base, time, and distance fare. On the other hand, Lyft may charge these extra fees in the form of a percentage that is added to the base ride amount. Therefore, if a prime time ride increase was 50%, then a ride that would normally cost $10 would go up to $15 during prime time. These surges for both companies occur during rush hour times and/or during some special events.

DRINKING AND RIDESHARE

Common sense would dictate that people would be less tempted to drink and drive if they have an easier, safer way to get home after a night out. It depends on the study. Uber makes its own case with this statement:

> *After the company rolled out its ride-sharing services in San Francisco in 2010, they reported declines in drunken driving incidents in several other major cities. They reference a study that shows a 3.6% to 5.6% decrease in drunk driving deaths in California.*
>
> Brad Greenwood, University of Minnesota and Sunil Wattal, Temple University, 2015

According to other statistics, the actual number of Uber and Lyft drivers on the road is still relatively small to credit them with making a serious dent in the more than 10,000 people who die annually in the United States in drunk driving collisions. With hundreds of thousands of Uber drivers on the clock each month, there are still 4.2 million people who choose to drive drunk every month (CDC, August 7, 2015). Still, more studies show that Uber and Lyft are having some positive effect. Another independent study in New York City shows a twenty-five to thirty-five percent decrease in drunk driving incidents since Uber started offering its services in 2011 © (Jessica Lynn Peck, CUNY Graduate Center, January 2017.) as opposed to other cities where Uber or Lyft do not operate.

When the concept of ride-share happened, many people came out against it for numerous reasons. Taxi drivers are one group who were outraged as their livelihood was threatened by this new, ideal product. However, below are some reasons why a drunk driver may choose to use a ride-share such as Uber or Lyft, instead of a taxi:

1. Opportunities for Free Rides. It depends on the location,but when Uber expands into a new city they will offer customers opportunities for free rides. Whether this offer is for a period of time in which all rides are free altogether or existing customers receive a promo code to get free first rides; it's undoubtedly a win-win for both the company and the consumer.

2. Drivers Earn Their Reputation. When an Uber ride is complete, the customer is asked to rate the driver and their ride share experience. You can rate such things as: cleanliness of the car, driver personality and overall ride impression. They also provide a section for the rider's comments. Uber drivers love it! They get to earn a good reputation amongst riders while new riders have an opportunity to be informed on who will be driving them before the driver arrives. If he or she doesn't like what they read, they can cancel the ride at no cost to them.

3. Greater Transparency. When you receive a receipt for a taxi trip, there often are a few prices, and, depending on the city/company, rarely a driver name. If a rider is new to a location, the trip could take a longer route than necessary, thus be charged a higher price. When using Uber, the app generates a receipt for the trip and tracks your route, so whether drunk or just new to a city, you can determine whether you have been taken advantage of.

4. It Costs Less. Some researchers suggest that drunk driving hasn't decreased in some cities that offer Uber or Lyft *(American Journal of Epidemiology, July 22, 2106)*. Some impaired drivers believe it's cheaper to take a chance driving drunk rather than pay for a taxi or use a ride-share service. This is contrary to the truth. In the vast majorityof cases, using Uber is between twenty-five to fifty percent cheaper than hiring a taxi, and although public transportation is inexpensive, often times it is unavailable in many cities. The savings can add up to a few drinks at the bar, buying one's date a dessert and, of course, being able to take Uber or Lyft to get home.

5. The Modern Technology. Although the price for basic service for both ride-share companies appear to be generally similar, I love how Uber and Lyft are parallel when it comes to the convenience and use of its technology. First, both companies allow a person to request a ride from their cell phone. When using the Uber or Lyft app a person can see what Uber or Lyft cars are in their area. Once a driver accepts the pickup, the rider gets an alert as to how long it will be before the driver arrives. Often someone who has been having lots of fun drinking can lose track of time. One of the beauties of using Uber or Lyft is that the app will alert the rider as to when the ride has arrived.

Within the US, ride-sharing for the most part is, for better or worse, the story of two competitors. In the US, Uber was and still is the more aggressive and dominant in the minds of most riders. However, Lyft, with its steady and constant business management strategies, has developed the reputation of a distant number two. They have enveloped twenty-three percent of the ride-share business in the country by offering discounts for those in need of a ride.

Lyft's recent moves within the sphere of ride-share has been to approach its business and work strategy to build a stronger reputation that won't be the equivalent of Uber's shadow. For instance, airlines have for some time now integrated rental cars into their airline promotional infrastructure. Lyft is now making the big move to offer Delta SkyMiles. With each dollar of a fare, the rider will be generating a Delta SkyMile mile. This is a great alternative for those people who drink alcohol, fly and need to continue their trip in a car to their final destination.

This offer may be particularly sweet in the state of Arizona because Lyft offers discounted rides to all Arizona State University (ASU) students and staff, many of whom come from out of state and use Lyft as a way of transport to and from the airport. The discounted deal is also a great deal for ASU students because it encourages students to use Lyft when out partying instead of getting behind the wheel of a car while intoxicated. This is vital when one considers how most college students behave at an age when they are likely to drink and drive.

Lyft is also teaming with Allscripts, a leading electronic health records company. Lyft plans to integrate its platform into the daily routines of 2,500 hospitals, 45,000 medical practices and 180,000 physicians and has the potential to reach an estimated seven million patients. A desktop app allows medical facilities to call multiple cars at once and send each patient their ride details via text message. Healthcare providers cover the cost of the ride unless otherwise specified.

As a driver for Uber and Lyft, I've experienced a wide range of personalities, many of whom are intoxicated. On a typical Friday or Saturday night, I pick up many people who have obviously been drinking at some point in the evening, whether before, during or after they head home. Out of curiosity, I ask many of my inebriated riders why they use Uber or Lyft. Most of the time, they state that they simply didn't want to drive drunk and/or describe a previous drunk driving experience.

I know we need ride-shares like Uber and Lyft. Uber and Lyft offer superior alternatives that maximize technology at a lesser cost. Ride-sharing is technology evolution that works. Statistics show that in many cases drunk driving is down in several cities where Uber *(Uber MADD Report 2015)* and Lyft operate. More research will need to be done. However, it's a great start to a better functioning society when it comes to drunk driving.

IN HIS OWN WORDS
Chris R.

I am telling my life story in hopes of stopping someone from ruining the lives of so many people, like I did. Whenever my family went on vacation, I remember my father driving with a beer between his legs. I remember him reaching his hand over the back seat; I would take the empty can and give him an unopened can of beer. This went on for many years. As a kid growing up, I remember there was always alcohol in my house. My father gave me a truck about the time I turned eighteen years old. Of all of my friends, I was the only one who had a car at the time. We would go looking for parties around town on Friday and Saturday nights. Just bring a cup ... they always had beer kegs.

I never thought about driving under the influence (DUI) until I got my first one at eighteen years old. About eight of my friends and I went out for a day at the river. Driving home that night, three guys sat in the front seat and five guys sat in the bed of my truck. I drove through a yellow light. The cop was waiting at the light. He pulled me over and issued me a ticket; I was convicted of my first DUI. I spent one night in jail and was court ordered to attend a DUI school for three months. All I remember about the DUI school was the conversations with the other students. Usually we talked about our weekend plans and exchanged strategies on how to avoid a future DUI ticket.

Arizona Department of Transportation

About six months later I was with a friend. Again, it was a Friday night and we were cruising down a popular boulevard. My friend made a comment to someone in another car that was also cruising. After a few *F bombs* were exchanged, we went our separate ways. Later that night we were looking for a backyard party. I pulled up to the house in my truck and the same guy who my friend talked crap to on the boulevard, saw my truck parked in front of the house party. The guy pulls my friend out of the passenger window. As all of this is happening the police pull up to the house. Since I was sitting in my truck in the middle of the road, I was charged with my second DUI.

I said to myself, "Man, you have some bad luck. You need to stop hanging around with those guys."

I paid my fine and did what the court ordered. I tried my best not to get into any more trouble. It worked for about six or seven years. I tried not to drive if I knew I would be drinking. When I did drink and drive it never crossed my mind that I could kill someone or myself. Worse case, I thought I would have some bad luck and have to pay a fine, go to traffic school again and/or maybe go to jail for a few days or weeks.

When I was attending my court-ordered A.A. meetings, I met a real pretty girl. She was very serious about staying sober. I ended up moving in with her, and it was not long before my girlfriend got pregnant. We got married. I was happy. I thought my life had finally started to work out great. My marriage was fine. It was after my daughter's birth when my marriage started to have problems. Looking back, I think my wife was suffering from depression. She made comments like, "I am too fat; you have a girlfriend."

I worked for a construction company. The owner would bid on jobs that were out of town a lot. If the job was going to take a while, the owner would rent a house for the crew and I would live there six days a week. I worked for the company for close to eighteen years. My wife was unhappy with me because the guys I worked with would drink beer every day after work. I would eat, drink, shower and go to bed. This was what I thought was a normal life because growing up, this is what I remember my father did.

One Friday night after being gone for the week, I drove home. When I arrived my wife and daughter were both gone. I asked her aunt and uncle if they knew my wife and daughter's whereabouts. They told me that they had not heard from them. It took me about a month before I was able to find my wife and daughter. I met them at a restaurant and attempted to save my marriage.

Consumed with emotions, I had signed a stack of papers without even reading them, which gave my wife permission to leave the state with our child. In a period of about one and a half years I received four DUIs. I was so unhappy. I wished that I was dead. The DUI that landed me in prison involved a car crash with a woman who was pregnant. I caused her to lose her baby. Because of my prior DUIs, I received a total sentence of twenty-two years to life for the death of the baby *plus* another seven years for injuring the woman.

This is my first prison term. I came to prison at the age of thirty-seven. I do not see the parole board until 2026. At that time, I will have to explain to them how I became the person who was sentenced and sent to prison. I have had many years to think about how I threw my life away. I had many poor role models growing up. I believe seeing my father drinking and driving made me think it was okay to drink and drive. Plus, all my friends were alcoholics. After seeing this alcoholic behavior for so many years it became a part of what I thought was a normal life. It was not until the criminal justice officials, parole board and counselors told me that if I didn't change my whole life style, I could just stay in prison for the rest of my life.

I work a Twelve-Step program. I am hoping the reader takes my advice. Remember you are already a marked man or woman with a DUI. It is so easy to get another one once you start drinking and driving. Use your imagination. When you drink, drive and get caught, you are going to be giving up your freedom to go wherever you want. You will also have to eat what you are served in prison. You have to shower and go to bed when you are told. You will constantly be with people you don't trust or even like. Once you receive a sentence of fifteen years to life for Second Degree Murder you will have to explain to the parole board how you allowed your life to become so messed up and what made you think it was safe to drink and drive.

To be released from prison after being sentenced is very difficult. You will have to prove to the parole board, by your actions and behavior, that you are no longer a threat to society. You must explain when your life started going off course and how you were able to fix it while in prison. They will have many questions for you to answer about your family life and what type of friends you had. Remember, it says *to life* at the end of your sentence. If the parole board feels you have not answered their questions properly, parole will not be granted.

Under California's Marsy's Law indeterminate inmates are given three, five, seven, ten or fifteen-year denials when found unsuitable for parole. Basically, being found unsuitable is equivalent to receiving a new sentence. One has to serve this amount of time before getting another opportunity. I have talked to people who were sentenced seven years to life who have been serving over thirty years in prison. It is the parole board's job to be sure that you will never hurt anyone again.

I am telling you this because at the time that I was drinking and driving, I thought I was not hurting anyone but myself. I did not realize how wrong my thoughts were until I was informed that I was being charged with murder. I thought murder meant I had to shoot or stab someone, not crashing a car. I learned that the car I was driving was the weapon.

I have only told you about the problems I experienced since I killed an innocent unborn baby. What about their loved ones? The person I killed would have grown up to be a father, a mother, brother or sister. Put yourself in their shoes and see all the needless suffering that could've been avoided, if I would have not decided to drink and drive. This goes for driving high on weed too.

Hopefully, the information I have shared about what can happen if you decide to drink and drive will make you stop and think, "Do I really want to go to prison for a long time and have the label of being a murderer for the rest of my life?"

If I could, I would put up a billboard everywhere that states, "If you drink and drive and kill someone, you will go to prison for at least fifteen years to life."

Thank you for *listening* to my message. Think before you drink or just stay home. It will save everyone a lot of pain and suffering.

IN HIS OWN WORDS
Eric

In October 2005, while driving intoxicated, I struck and killed a police officer as he was conducting a freeway closure shortly after four o'clock in the morning. He was twenty-nine years old.

I made the choice to drive intoxicated despite knowing the dangers of driving under the influence (DUI) and being warned by others that I was too intoxicated to drive that night. I did not have to make this choice. I could have drunk responsibly. I could have taken a cab home. I could have slept at a friend's house. There were thousands of choices I could have made that night instead of driving home intoxicated. Yet, I selfishly chose to disregard the danger of my actions, because it was too inconvenient for me to leave my car overnight at a bar. I am ashamed of my actions and their ongoing consequences. My hope is that this testimonial will persuade others with similar problems to take the necessary steps to address their underlying issues with alcohol and the choices they make while intoxicated.

When I was seventeen years old I took my first drink of alcohol. It was from a bottle of wine that I shared with a friend on a beach. Afterwards, we stumbled to his car and my friend drove us home while I played with the radio. When we reached my house, I crept up my driveway like a cat burglar, tiptoeing up the walkway as my friend looked on laughing. When I reached my front door, I peeked through a side window and turned back to give my friend an enthusiastic thumbs up. He nodded his head and drove off as I slid inside, sneaking past my parent's bedroom door into my room where I collapsed onto my bed.

I felt like I had just gotten away with something, and I had. My friend and I had not only drunk underage but had driven home intoxicated. It was an hour and a half drive from the beach to where I lived with my parents. Our choice to drive intoxicated put everyone we encountered along the way at risk. I should have recognized the danger we created. Unfortunately, I felt no regret or fear; that would come later. Instead, I had a memory of a fun night with a friend, along with a newly formed belief that alcohol can take an ordinary night and make it extraordinary.

My drinking progressed after I entered the military. Now drinking wasn't just about having fun, it was a means of validating myself. I was tough if I could drink a lot of alcohol. It was *cool* to be seen with my friends at a bar with a drink in my hand. As shallow and self-centered as those pursuits were, they mattered to me, so I sought them out.

I had many justifications for my actions. I always focused on certain areas of my life to convince myself that I was a good person. I told myself, I didn't have an alcohol problem because I never got a DUI, and because I was only a social drinker. Over time, my beliefs grew more dysfunctional as I continued drinking and making dangerous choices while intoxicated. I believed that drinking and driving was wrong when other people did it, but not me.

"I was a *good* driver; I was different; I didn't have a drinking problem. Nothing like the thousands of deaths caused by impaired driving every year could happen to someone like me; I'm a good person." It is

> **Heavy alcohol use is a significant problem in the military. Personnel often use alcohol in an attempt to cope with stress, boredom, loneliness, and the lack of other recreational activities.**
>
> *Genevieve Ames, Ph.D. and Carol Cunradi, M.P.H., Ph.D. National Institute on Alcohol Abuse and Alcoholism*

shameful for someone to believe that his/her actions will not harm others simply because that person thinks him/herself to be important or special. I was that person.

I could have learned a lot from the officer. He had only been an officer four short-years; yet, he accomplished so much. On one occasion, he saved a man's life who was pinned under a car. He lifted the car from the man's chest in order for him to breathe, and then held it there until help arrived. He received the *Life Saving Effort Award* and the *Medal of Valor*. In 2004, he was awarded the Mothers Against Drunk Driver's (MADD) *Hero Award* for making the most driving under the influence (DUI) arrests in the county. He was the department's most productive officer and a member of the Special Weapons and

Tactical Team (SWAT).

I was nothing like him. When I came back from deployments in the military, I brought back a sense of entitlement. I only thought of the things I felt others owed me, never about the responsibility I had to other people or my community. My life stood in stark contrast to the officer's life. I used my service in the military to justify my inexcusable behavior. I invested myself into drinking and partying. I was shallow and selfish. I put off my responsibilities in life, so I could have my time. I never thought about anyone else.

Had I exercised the least bit of care or willingness to reflect on my character and actions, the officer's life would not have been cut short. During my sentencing, many people testified about his character. They spoke how he positively affected their lives and the entire community. Every day he wore his uniform he put his life on the line with a sense of responsibility and gratitude towards his job and the people he served. He was the good person I pretended to be.

If you are reading this testimonial and have made the choice to drive while intoxicated, then it is critical that you take an honest look at your substance use and the choices you are making. Whether it be in *Responsibly Driven,* Alcoholics Anonymous (A.A.), substance abuse treatment, or through trusted friends and family, please get the help you need to ensure that you never find yourself behind the wheel while intoxicated. Deaths caused by driving under the influence are preventable. Your life and the lives of those who live in your community depend on it.

IN HIS OWN WORDS
A Law Enforcement Officer

I was new on the job, less than a year in fact. Although early into my graveyard shift, it was late at night, sometime just after 12 am. My partner and I were on a stop, and I was in the middle of writing a citation when we got the call of a wrong-way driver traveling south in the northbound lanes of the road. My partner, an officer with five years of service, told me I'd better hurry up, because we had to go. I quickly finished with the driver, jumped in the car, and we headed out.

As soon as we hit the northbound road, dispatch updated us on the wrong-way driver; it was witnessed still heading southbound. My partner turned to me and said something about the driver probably crashing at some point. Knowing I would be taking the report, I began to get nervous, and started to prioritize the things I would need to do in my head if he had crashed. About a minute passed when dispatch came over the radio to say the vehicle had crashed, and that there were possibly two other cars involved. I tried to prepare myself for what I expected to see; only I had no idea what to expect.

When we arrived on the scene, the first vehicle I came upon was a crumpled mass of smoking metal. The driver's head was stuck in the windshield, which had split it open enough to expose his brain. He was slowly opening and closing his mouth as red foam came out, due to what I could only assume was at least one punctured lung. He was dead within minutes. His front passenger at least had the forethought to put on his seatbelt before getting on the road in the wrong direction, a move that most likely saved his life. He was broken, but he was alive. What we did not know at the time and found out while at the hospital some time later was that there was a third person in that vehicle.

The rear passenger was jammed so far under the seats in the back that he went unseen until the tow trucks arrived. He most likely died on impact. Earlier that day, the three of them had finished work at one of the local ranches and proceeded to drink the three eighteen-packs of beer they had with them. This was learned a few days later when we interviewed the surviving front passenger. After finishing off those beers, one of them drove to the store and bought three more eighteen-packs. He then drove back to the location where they were drinking, a side road off the main road, a few miles from town.

The evidence of empty scattered beer cans was discovered the next day by a passing driver who saw the cans reflecting in the sunlight just off the road. Knowing about the collision from the news reports he watched that morning, and realizing that he was near the scene, he pulled off the road to further investigate the reflections and found the scattered cans and empty containers. According to the results of an autopsy, the driver was found to be three times the legal limit at the time of the collision.

In the other patrol unit on scene were two officers with whom I graduated from the law enforcement academy. I saw they were assisting the five occupants in the van, so I ran back to the last vehicle. There were five family members in that car. Most were only shaken up as the car was only sideswiped by the wrong-way car.

After I calmed them down and obtained some information, I went back to the van to help my partners. I could see where the driver had taken the majority of the impact. The collision shoved the engine block into his legs, which in turn, pushed his seat into the girl sitting behind him. They were both trapped in the van until fire personnel were able to free them. There was also a young man and woman in the back seat who managed to get themselves out through the rear of the vehicle.

They were all just kids. It was a van full of teenagers from a Christian high school on their way to a retreat. The driver was a football star, who had just scored a touchdown in the game that night. I learned this fact from talking with his mom at the hospital that night. He lost one of his legs in the crash. The girl sitting behind him was a cheerleader for the team. She died at the hospital. The driver's father was sitting in the front seat of the van, and aside from cuts and contusions, he seemed to be alright. While at the hospital that night, I spent some time with the family and their pastor. These were good people, God loving and devoted to one another. They made a huge impact on me that night. I truly shared in their pain. I was later invited to speak at an assembly when the driver returned to school and had the chance to see the kids again, but under much better circumstances.

A few days following the crash, my partners, our dispatcher, sergeant and myself attended a group counselling session. It was helpful and somewhat comforting when I learned my buddies were having the same feelings I was experiencing. It still stings a bit when I think about that night, but I manage to push through it along with the rest of the painful memories from my sixteen year career.

IN HER OWN WORDS
Heather

In 2007, I was losing my battle with alcoholism and drug addiction while dealing with three mental health disorders: bi-polar, anxiety and post-traumatic stress disorder (PTSD). I lived my life in survival mode because that was the only way I chose to deal with my past issues. My father taught me how to be a drunk and an addict at an early age. I told myself that I would never be like him, and I wasn't. I became something much worse that tragic night I killed an innocent woman while driving under the influence of alcohol.

I grew up in a very toxic environment. Both of my parents were addicts and criminals and very neglectful toward my siblings and I. My father was verbally, emotionally, physically and sexually abusive. He also tortured us by killing our pets. The majority of day, my father locked himself in his bedroom to do drugs. At the age of five, my mother was murdered while I played in the next room. To say the least, my youthful days were full of neglect, substance abuse, violence and fear.

As a result of these traumatic experiences, I didn't function as a normal kid. My family refused to believe anything was wrong with me. I was haunted by my feelings of anger, sadness, guilt, shame, worthlessness and fear. In order to maintain some semblance of well-being, I began to self-medicate with alcohol and drugs. To find happiness, I jumped from man to man. I foolishly believed I would find the contentment my soul yearned. Most of the time, I settled for the empty feeling of inebriated numbness. Eventually, the severity of my addition and destructive behaviors increased. I also hid my demons as I grew older. I instantly denied that I had any problems. I chose to suffer alone. Sadly, it wasn't until the age of twenty-seven that I finally received a proper psychological diagnosis.

Everything culminated that tragic night. I had constantly struggled to pay my bills, which was largely due to my addictive lifestyle. As a consequence, I regularly could not afford to buy my psychotropic medication, so my days had turned into a quest of escape. The combination of addiction, mental illness and irresponsibility transformed me into a ticking timebomb. I accelerated that timer once I bought a car. I did not consider the dangers of impaired driving. Actually, I didn't care; I drove impaired all the time. I was arrested for both of my DUI (driving under the influence) tickets driving out of a bar's parking lot.

Wyoming Governor's Council on Impaired Driving

Moreover, I refused to attend the court-ordered DUI classes and Alcoholic Anonymous (A.A.) meetings. My DUI homicide was the inevitable culmination of my selfish and immature lifestyle.

On the day of the fatal auto collision I had a bad cold. In fact, I could hardly even speak and barely had any voice left. Nevertheless, I still decided to pick up my friend/co-worker from work. We worked at a restaurant in an outdoor mall, which had many other bars and restaurants. When I arrived she was sitting at the bar drinking, already on her way to becoming drunk. I joined her and ordered a strong alcoholic beverage. We then had a couple drinks and split a pizza. This sort of outing was common. She and I went out a lot and drank together often. This particular time we stayed at the restaurant for a few hours.

Initially, I took her home, naïvely believing that it was no big deal since she only lived ten minutes away from the restaurant. When I dropped her off I thought to myself, "Wow, she's really drunk!" However, I thought that I was okay to drive. Reflecting back on the severity of my intoxication, it makes me sick to my stomach that I decided to continue to drive. Also, it really freaks me out thinking about the extent of my denial. I already had two DUI convictions and one alcohol-related collision. I was lucky enough to live through that collision after knocking down a light pole. Fortunately, no one was hurt, except me. Yet, after those prior drunk driving experiences, here I was again, driving heavily impaired.

By the time I finally dropped off my friend at her home it was past midnight. Afterwards I headed toward the freeway on my way to my sister's house. Once I exited the freeway I drove down a boulevard for a few miles. There were hardly any cars on the street. The boulevard became very dark as I passed a theme park's parking lot. There were no streets or sidewalks. Since it had been previously raining, my car's windshield had raindrop spots on it. To make matters worse, my car's headlights were ineffectively dim. Combine these factors with intoxication and my previous DUI experience, there was no way that I should have been driving.

I did not see anything in front of me, but suddenly something cracked my windshield. I hadn't a clue what I hit. It seemed like something just fell out of the sky. Terrified of the unknown, I didn't stop to see what hit my windshield. I should have stopped, but like many other choices that I made that night, I failed to make the right one. I wish I would have stopped right away. If I had stopped, maybe the innocent woman's life would have been spared.

Instead of stopping, I kept driving until I reached a shopping center. I parked under the sign of one of its stores with my car facing the street. When I got out of my car to inspect the damage, I noticed that my windshield was caved in and had a huge hole.

In the past, I always looked to someone else to fix my problems. I needed someone to tell me what to do, so in a panic, I used my phone to call for help. As I placed multiple calls, I walked back down the street to see if I could see what I hit. I walked quite far, because I didn't realize how far I had driven from the collision. Since, I still couldn't see anything that I might have hit, I turned around and walked back to my car.

I finally reached someone on the phone, my ex-fiancé. Still very agitated, I began to yell at him. I don't remember exactly what he told me, but he did advise me to call the police. I did not heed his advice. Again, I failed to do the right thing.

A tow truck driver drove up to me as I was talking to my ex-fiancé. He saw me yelling on the phone from across the street. After a brief conversation, I jumped into his tow truck and returned to the collision scene. There were police cars and a fire truck at the collision site by the time we arrived. Once I saw them, I realized something really bad had happened.

No one ever thinks that they could kill somebody by drinking and driving; I didn't think that I would hurt, let alone kill anybody. Furthermore, I felt invincible. Irrespective of my traumatic past, I felt like nothing bad could ever happen to me. I never wanted to hurt anybody. I didn't want someone to suffer because of my actions. Many of my decisions were based with this distorted thinking. The reality was that my destructive lifestyle was hurting many people, even before this tragic night.

When the police officer informed me that I had hit a lady on a bicycle, my heart dropped. He admonished me for not stopping to render aid or to call the police. He felt that I fled the collision scene and tried to get away. He scolded me by telling me that I was a selfish person who only thinks of herself. He was right!

After being questioned for some time, I was handcuffed and then arrested. Just before being driven to the police station, I was informed that the lady died a half hour after arriving at the emergency room. In that moment I began to question myself, "How did this happen?" and wished that I could rewind the whole night. I wished I had made different decisions. But, I didn't, and a woman lost her life and her family was forever impacted.

While at the police station the officers finished their interrogation and booking process. They then transferred me to the county jail. I was eventually charged with Gross Vehicular Manslaughter while Intoxicated with a prior DUI conviction and Failure to Stop at the Scene of an Injury Accident, also known as Hit and Run. In that moment, while sitting in a two-person cell, I struggled to comprehend what had just happened. For hours, I blankly stared into the distance completely forlorn, shocked, and confused. Regrettably, the state of confusion lingered for years.

Two and half years lapsed before my trial began. Being in complete denial, I continued the court proceedings because I genuinely felt that I was not completely at fault and did not deserve a prison sentence. My thought process and emotional state had been erratic since my youth; sober or intoxicated. Those two years of continuances were a prime example of how I was still thinking irrational. Another example of my irrationality was my rejection of the District Attorney's (DA) plea bargain of a determinative fifteen-year sentence.

I foolishly believed that I was not guilty of Second Degree Murder.

Throughout this whole ordeal the gravity of the tragedy weighed on me. I heavily medicated myself with psychotropic drugs to feel numb. My zombie-like appearance in court left the impression that I didn't care, but that wasn't true. I was falling apart, and I needed an escape. I killed a mother of four children. I knew how it felt to unjustly lose one's mother. The traumatic experience of my mother's murder profoundly affected me, so I took it deeply to heart that I was the cause of someone else losing their mother. Today, this reality continues to devastate me.

After I rejected the DA's plea bargain, my trial began. I lost my trial. Once again in denial, I could not believe it. Two months later, I was sentenced to twenty years to life. During my sentencing hearing, I had my defense attorney read a letter that I wrote the judge. I felt so ashamed and embarrassed when I read the letter years later. It was superficial, self-centered and self-serving.

Now, I realize that my intention for writing that letter was to solicit sympathy. I desperately wanted people to see me as a victim. I was so wrong! It took incarceration and five years of group therapy for me to finally realize just how badly I'd behaved and to understand how society viewed me. I was a danger to society. The way that I was living my life, it was inevitable that I ended up killing somebody while driving impaired. The reality was I was a killer waiting to *unload my gun.*

Today, I am a different person. This experience has humbled me. It's been hard dealing with the shame and guilt of this lady's murder and its unmeasurable impact, the loss of many relationships and freedom, the plaguing loneliness, and the lack of proper mental health care. Nevertheless, I've learned to let go of my past and learned to love myself. I used to let my past continue to victimize me. Although my mental health has been a rollercoaster ride, I don't drink alcohol or use drugs to cope. I still take prescription medicine to keep me stable, but my mental well-being is in a very good place. Most importantly, I love myself today.

One thing is for sure, I will never drive impaired again! There is too much to lose. Lives are at stake. I killed an innocent woman and destroyed her family. There is nothing I can say or do that will bring her back or comfort her family. Today, I'm making living amends by staying sober, living responsibly, and sharing my story. I plan to continue combating impaired driving for the rest of my life by speaking about my experience with impaired driving and its horrific consequences. If Mothers Against Drunk Drivers (MADD) would allow me to sit on a panel and share my insights, I am very willing. With that said, I pray daily for peace and healing for the woman's family. I truly hope they find a little solace one day.

    Drinking and driving is a horrible crime. It is my wish that my story will raise awareness about its deadly impact. Too many people are dying from impaired driving. The worst part is that it can be prevented. Moreover, I hope you, the reader, will learn from my mistakes. If you struggle with past traumatic experiences and/or mental health issues, ask for help! Don't let someone convince you that nothing is wrong. There are people and organizations that are eager to assist. You are important! Value your life! Please learn from my story. I do not want you or another family to suffer a similar fate.

IN HIS OWN WORDS
Douglas

My irresponsible and careless habit of driving under the influence (DUI) started back in the seventies while attending high school. I was part of the party crowd, so to speak. Among our social group, drinking and driving was the norm and accepted as an everyday occurrence. We all drove and rode in our cars and trucks while drinking; some of us on a daily basis. It was routine for my circle of friends to be driving while having a beer between our legs going to and from school, work, social gatherings, sporting events, etc.

Tragically, drinking and driving *back then* was treated much differently than today; not only amongst friends, but by law enforcement as well. Back then, even though we were not old enough to drink legally, law enforcement pulled us over on more than one occasion. Due to alcohol in our possession and driving under the influence, we were simply told, "Take it home." If we were stopped later, we would then be taken to jail.

Throughout high school, my friends and me wrecked our cars and trucks due to our drinking and driving. We would simply pick up the pieces and go about fixing or replacing our cars and trucks without giving our careless behavior a second thought. It was just part of life. Unfortunately, this irresponsible behavior carried into our adult lives.

After high school, I started working in the construction trade. Driving with a beer between my legs was still normal and accepted as routine. Every day after work, my co-workers and I would crack a few beers while still on the job site and then review the day before driving home for dinner. For some, drinking a couple of beers went from the job site and moved to a bar for a few more. Wrecking our cars and trucks continued; the behavior wasn't given a second thought. We all had stories to tell. Our drinking, driving and wrecks were to some degree considered bragging rights.

Even the music we listened to glorified our irresponsible drinking and driving. I remember one song, written by Lynard Skynard and titled *That Smell,* contained the lyrics: "Whiskey bottles, brand new cars, oak tree you're in my way" *(Street Survivors, 1977).*

The road to my life sentence for vehicular manslaughter started when I first got my license to drive. In 1987, while under the influence of alcohol, I drove my truck head-on into another vehicle, instantly killing its driver. Raised in a small mountain town, I knew the person I killed. She was the mother of two schoolmates who I considered friends. She was also my son's kindergarten teacher.

I woke up in the hospital handcuffed to the bed and was soon transferred to county jail where I was charged with Gross Vehicular Manslaughter. Since it was my first time in trouble, the courts were relatively easy on me for my careless and irresponsible actions. I was sentenced to eighteen months in county jail, one year in a live-in alcohol and drug program and ten years in prison suspended if I would complete a five year probation period successfully.

> The fee to cover the average incarceration for Federal inmates in Fiscal Year 2015 was $31,977.65, or $87.61 per day.
>
> *Federal Register: Annual Determination of Average Cost of Incarceration 7/19/2016*

I completed the eighteen months in county jail and the one year in rehab. I did not take my rehab seriously enough nor the tragedy that I caused. In my fourth year of probation, I got into a car again with an open container of wine. I violated my terms of probation and was sent to prison to serve the ten years.

Upon my release from prison and still not understanding the seriousness of my past actions, I found myself back in prison on alcohol-related charges. This became a pattern with me. My selfish and irresponsible behavior continued and lead to a life sentence. Alcohol was involved every time I was sent back to prison. I was an alcoholic and needed to stop drinking. I attended A.A. meetings, but I did not work the steps. I thought to myself, "Why isn't this A.A. stuff working for me?" and became disappointed with the program.

Coming out of prison for the fourth time, I took the required DUI course to get my license back. Not having learned my lesson, I was arrested for DUI again and was on my way back to prison for the fifth and final time. *Three strikes and I'm out.* I received a sentence of twenty-five years to life, even though there was no collision or injury. The sentence was for my repeated reckless behavior. Game over.

Sadly, after numerous opportunities to change my careless behavior, I didn't get it until I was handed a life sentence. Since incarceration, I started attending the A.A. program, applied myself and did the work on each step of the program. I can honestly say that for the first time in my alcoholism, I have no desire to drink what so ever. I owe it to God and the A.A. program for removing that desire. It may be a little late for me, but not for you.

So, *listen* up! Don't end up like me. My story is a warning to you – don't disregard the precious opportunity to change the road on which you may be headed that could lead to a collision because of drinking and driving. Causing someone's death is a nightmare from which you never wake up. The guilt and shame of taking a human life is difficult to live with on a daily basis. Not only did my irresponsible and careless behavior take a human life, but it affected dozens of people. Kids without a mother, grandkids without a grandmother; as well as what it did to my family without me as a father. Literally, dozens of people from both families are impacted in a negative manner because of my reckless actions.

So, ask yourself, if you are willing to live with the tragic consequences of DUI the next time you decide to get in your car or truck while intoxicated?

IN HIS OWN WORDS
Chris M.

There is a way that seems right to a man, But its end is the way of death.
Proverbs 14:12 (NASB)

Perhaps my way on this path began when I got drunk for the first time at the age of five during a family get together. I went around taking sips from the guests' alcoholic drinks as they laughed and patted me on the head, thinking it was funny. I remember them saying, *"like father, like son."* I felt accepted drinking with the grown-ups. Thus, began a life saturated with alcohol.

Alcohol was such a part of my family life that I thought it was normal. My father drank anytime he was home from work. I believed this behavior was part of *being a man.* When he allowed me to sit in his lap and watch television, he would let me take sips of his beer until I fell asleep and then carried me to bed. I felt loved and cherished. Later in life, my dad would take my friends and I snake hunting. My dad always brought beer along on these forays. One time, I remember a Highway Patrol officer pulled my dad over for swerving. My dad flashed his sheriff's badge and the officer let him go saying, "Drive straight home, you've had too much to drink" I never realized we were in any danger or that my dad was breaking the law. When you're a kid no matter how messed up life is you believe everything is normal. I came to believe driving impaired was an acceptable behavior.

In the fourth grade, a couple of friends and I skipped school and went to a friend's house. We broke into his dad's liquor cabinet. I thought it was an adventure and that I was brave and bold. When the kids at school heard what we had done, I felt like they looked up to us. It was the first time I felt like one of the cool kids.

In junior high school, I had a friend who lived with his

older brothers. His house was a hangout for the party crowd. When I started drinking with the older kids, I became excited to be included in their scene. Although I felt too shy to talk to the pretty high school girls, I found that alcohol gave me a false sense of confidence. I believed that I was becoming an adult by doing adult things when I drank. In high school, it was a party on wheels. I lived for the weekends. As a successful athlete, I wanted to show my manhood by drinking, fighting, and hooking up with girls. This was my idea of a *teenage high life*.

I didn't realize how addiction impeded my development and maturity. I foolishly believed that alcohol had been a positive factor in my life. It had been a support, helper, facilitator and friend. Nearly every television program that I watched in the seventies showed adults drinking alcohol and smoking tobacco. My hero, John Wayne, would walk into a bar, throw back a few shots of whiskey, fight the whole bar, and then walk out with a good-looking woman on his arm. I didn't realize alcohol's negative impact on my life.

On the home front, things were not going well. My dad had a new job working as a prison guard for the Sheriff's Department and began working a lot of overtime. He also began to drink a lot more. The relationship between my mom and dad got worse. They began fighting more as my dad's drinking increased. Their arguments became physical as my dad beat my mom. I was scared and didn't understand the reasons my dad was acting so mean. The family began to fear when he had a day off. I remember my mom pleading with him to stop drinking, but he would simply say, "It's a man's right to drink."

He believed if he worked hard, that he was entitled to drink and relax and that no woman was going to *control him* by denying him that right. I took these words to heart thinking this was all part of being a man, but I didn't like the fact that he hit my mom. This became a poison dart in my relationship with my dad. I started covering my mom during his drunken attacks. I also began weight training to get strong enough to defend my mom. My dad's drinking got so bad that he even started attacking us kids.

As this was happening, my friends became more and more important to me. The party scene was an escape from my troubled home life. I didn't know how to handle what was happening at home. I couldn't fix things, so alcohol became a way to dull the emotional pain. I didn't know my alcoholism was growing into a six-hundred-pound *beast* that would become my worst enemy.

One day when I was fifteen years old my dad was drinking. He thought I disrespected him, so he attacked me. By now, I had become strong enough to defend myself, so I body-slammed him and knocked him out. I knew I had crossed a line. Sure enough, when my dad became conscious, he kicked me out of his house and told me never to return. I immediately packed my bags and left home.

I went to my friend's house (the one who lived with his older brothers), but they told me they couldn't support me and that I needed to find a job to support myself if I wanted to live with them. My friend and I found jobs with a traveling carnival. We dropped out of high school and took off with the company.

We traveled throughout the central states for eight months, working fourteen-hour days and partying ten-hour nights. I learned how to drink every day. One day while working the carnival in Wyoming my mom showed up to inform me that she was divorcing my dad and that she needed me to go with her to Michigan to help raise my siblings. I was more than ready to leave the *carney* life behind. I saw that drugs and alcohol caused stabbings, beatings, and killings. It scared me. I knew I needed to return to high school if I wanted to have a better life than I had experienced as a carnival worker.

Life in small town Michigan was a drastic change for me, especially after having lived such a wild life on my own. Despite the challenges, I settled into high school and received good grades. Yet, the *beast* seemed to be everywhere. It was in the cases of beer left on my grandmother's porch. It was in the comradery drinking of the lumberjacks where I worked. The *beast* was at the keg parties with my high school friends. In any uncertainty or insecurity, difficulty or struggle, pain or affliction, the *beast* was there to help. Yet, I still didn't know that the *beast,* known as alcoholism, was taking me over.

After high school, I attended a university in Michigan. I moved into a fraternity house, got a job working fast food, and went to class full-time carrying sixteen units. It was the wild life all over again with its competitive drinking and marathon partying. It reminded me of the movie *Animal House,* starring John Belushi, who died of an alcohol and drug overdose.

My drinking had not caused any grave consequences in the beginning, but within two years of living an inebriated lifestyle, my grades suffered, and I was forced to drop out. I became ashamed of myself and failed to understand how the other men were able to handle the lifestyle we lived. It never occurred to me that my drinking was the cause of all my problems. I still couldn't see the *beast* for what it was!

I decided to move out west near my dad and find work in the construction trade. The economy in California was booming. I loved the familiar smell of sawdust, but I also loved the drinking culture that accompanied the trade. Again, I gravitated toward situations that would support my need for *drafts of fuel,* an integral part of my daily life. The foreman himself would supply us with the beer. If he thought we were becoming too intoxicated to work, but were doing a good job, he'd call it a day. This foreman eventually became my best friend, and sadly, was my car passenger during my fatal collision.

Apartment living can be expensive for a young twenty year old, so I moved into a nice five-bedroom house with a bunch of construction workers to split the rent. It was almost like living at the frat house, but I had no academic tests to pass. I didn't think that showing up hungover for my job and living with four other guys was a problem. However, the arrangement became a problem once a drug dealer, a friend of one of the workmen, moved in with us.

He didn't have to work because he shared all his profit from his drug trade with us. Within two weeks, I quickly developed a cocaine addiction that was out of control. Fortunately, the girl I was dating allowed me to move in with her; subsequently, I was able to stop using cocaine. I learned that cocaine was bad news and it could lead to an overdose, addiction, or even death. Regardless of this knowledge, I continued rationalizing my drinking. My girlfriend and I eventually got married and had two sons.

I finally saw the *beast* for what it was when a tragic family incident occurred. My little brother killed himself with a shotgun shot to his head. He was only fifteen years old. I flew to my mom's home in Michigan for his funeral. I found out he had been drinking the night he died. I felt guilty because I taught him how to drink; his first experience with alcohol was with me. Even though it was a closed casket visitation service,

I couldn't bear to go inside the mortuary. It so happened that a bar was across the street. Instead of attending the service, I took shelter in the bar. I knew about addiction, because of my stint with cocaine, but alcoholism was a whole different *beast*. I just couldn't stop using this substance!

Ironically, after my brother's death, in my self-hatred, I embraced the *beast*. I began drinking twenty-four/seven to block out the pain and to dull the memories. I was out of control and couldn't stop drinking alcohol, even though I tried. After receiving three DUIs in one year, I still

Jim Sullivan/J. Sullivan Productions

wouldn't admit that I had a problem. In part, I couldn't bear the thought of life without alcohol. Such a thought was simply too terrifying. At times, I thought the *beast* was helping me through the tough times. In reality, it was just crushing me and disempowering me even more. I deluded myself into thinking that I could master alcoholism on my own.

My wife divorced me when I went to county jail for eleven months. Even then, I wouldn't admit that alcohol was the cause of my problems. The *beast* had his big ugly hands over my eyes. The disease of alcoholism permeated and poisoned all of my senses. Alcohol was so much a part of my life and so ingrained into my psyche, I thought, "How can I have a problem with something that is as important as breathing? Living without it would be like walking without legs, singing without a voice, or hearing without ears. How would I be accepted by my friends? How can I stop drinking then show up to work and refuse to drink with my co-workers?"

I believed my character was too weak. I worried too much about what people would think of me. At the time, I didn't realize that if they were truly my friends, they'd completely understand what I was going through and support my efforts to live a sober life.

Then my dad said the most hurtful thing to me about my drinking, "What the hell is wrong with you? Why can't you handle your *mud?* You are nothing but a weak-willed p***y!"

That comment haunted my thoughts. It sapped and crippled my remaining strength. In my deformed thinking, I thought that I had to strive to overcome my weak will and to master alcohol. Anything else would be admitting defeat and being less of a man.

At one point, I was court-ordered to attend Alcoholics Anonymous (A.A.) for twenty years; yet, sobriety never made sense to me because I could not face the possibility of living my life without alcohol. I never worked A.A.'s Twelve-Steps until I came to prison and started seeking a Christian life. That's when I had a paradigm shift. I came to understand that A.A. is a Christian program. I surrendered my life, mind, heart and soul to God and asked for His help. (Note: In order to be politically correct, A.A. uses the term *Higher Power* instead of God, and that's cool with me. But in my experience the power rests only in a real relationship with the Living God.).

My son's birthday party was the night before my fatal DUI collision. I drank with my friends until the early morning hours. I had very little sleep, but having to take my friends home, I got up. I took a quick shower and flew out the door and into my car. The last thing I remembered was stepping on the gas to make it through a yellow light. I didn't see anyone approaching. I hit a van on the driver's side door, killing a woman instantly. She was a mother of four children and a grandmother. My self-centered, hedonistic lifestyle and addiction cost that woman her life. This was the second death that I blame myself and alcoholism.

There is no excuse for my actions. I had a lifetime of excuses as to why I drank, but now I have faced reality. I am guilty of DUI murder. I will live with the death of an innocent woman on my conscience for the rest of my life. Because of my decision to drive impaired, I was sentenced to fifteen years to life for DUI murder, plus an additional fifteen years to life sentence for Great Bodily Injury (GBI) to my passenger, and seven years for speeding.

It has taken twenty-five years of misery, two failed marriages, sadly two deaths, and a long prison sentence to wake me up to the truth about my problem. I hit rock bottom. My choices were suicide or complete surrender to God. I chose to surrender to God. Only then was I willing and able to start exploring the ways of living a sober life. With God's grace, I now have armor and weapons (provided by God and A.A.)

– insight, understanding, and discipline. I have tools to fight off any internal and external *beasts,* thoughts and feelings or circumstances that may afflict or prevent me from living life with clear eyes, an open heart, and a sober mind.

IN HIS OWN WORDS
Edward, DUI Counselor

It has been a humbling honor and privilege to be a part of this project. My name is Edward and I am a Certified Addiction Treatment Counselor (CATC II). For the past three years I have worked for Lucky Deuce's DUI Program, in beautiful Northern California. Prior to finding my passion in DUI (driving under the influence) work, I worked as a counselor at various residential treatment facilities. That experience provided me with a strong foundation for DUI prevention.

Over a year ago, Lucky Deuce DUI School received a random letter with a Soledad State Prison return address. I did not know why I was lead to open the envelope, but I did. My entire reason for working in a DUI program changed in that moment. Inside I found three poorly copied testimonials, written by prisoners who were doing life sentences for DUI homicide convictions. That evening I read the first testimonial, a rather long letter written by Chris M., to one of my DUI classes. The participants immediately had questions. What, when and how?

During the next group session, I read the other two testimonials. Once again the participants had questions. This time I wrote the questions down. I read all three

testimonies in each of the groups I facilitated and recorded their questions. Fortunately, Chris included his return address, so I sent him the participants' questions. A week or so later he answered their questions. We were the first agency to respond to him with questions. After a few letters back and forth, Chris invited me to help with this project.

DUI counselors, you may understand when I say that some of our curricula can be somewhat dry. I personally prefer facilitating with excitement and passion. These first three letters gave me that glimmer of something different, something real and something very relevant.

Fast forward several months, other DUI testimonials were sent to the school. What started with a few guys at Soledad prison, took on a life of its own. Through the *Responsibly Driven* program, the message got out. The school started receiving letters from other prisons besides Soledad. My role in this project has been to read the testimonials to my classes, inquire into their relevance and record the participants' reactions. My baseline question to the DUI class participants is, "Did the testimonial make you consider your actions?" Since I couldn't spend all my time reading the testimonials, I forwarded them onto my co-workers. I also shared them with our coastal agency location.

When a participant graduates from the DUI program, we ask them what part of the program had the most impact: the movie they watched; one of the assignments, etc.? Invariably, most participants say the testimonials *stuck out* the most. Just like our participants who come from various walks of life, these testimonials offer different perspectives on DUI. Some testimonials appeal to younger people, while others appeal to older people. Nevertheless, these stories speak volumes. I hope you find meaning in the words you read. I dearly wish that something in these testimonials resonates and possibly turns a life-changing bad decision into a series of lifelong good decisions.

When reading these testimonials, ask questions, or better yet, ask for questions. I have found that the obvious, "What is prison like?" type questions are not sufficient. My groups have gone deeper. My participants looked for insight into self-forgiveness, denial, familial/social support, genetic pre-disposition, grief, anger, and remorse, just to name a few topics. Challenge your participants to identify insightful connections to past behavior and discover social ways to improve their life.

IN HIS OWN WORDS
David L.

My name is Dave, and I am serving a life sentence for drinking and driving. My life did not have to turn out this way if only I would have heeded all the warnings. I grew up in a small town where everyone in high school would go out to a secluded area in the country and drink alcohol. Looking back over my life this is where I developed a bad habit and did not realize the harm I would eventually cause.

In high school, it started out with only drinking alcohol on the weekends. Through college I would drink anytime I got bored as I was looking for something to do. Over the years, I continued to drown myself with alcohol looking for what I thought was a good time.

My first DUI happened in 1999 when I worked as a truck driver hauling wastewater. A friend accompanied me so I wouldn't be bored driving overnight. We decided it was a good idea to bring some alcohol on the trip.

I didn't slow down in enough time to stop at a stop sign and rolled the diesel truck into a ditch. The impact caused my friend to become pinned inside the truck. As a result, he broke his leg and I went to jail. First Warning: alcohol impairs your judgement and your reflexes are slowed-down.

I went to court, lost my driving privileges, got fined, and had to live at a rehabilitation home for a year until my jail sentence was complete. I served my year, paid my fines, attended DUI classes for three months; then my driver's license was returned.

It is now 2001. I was out drinking with some of my friends at a party, but it was getting late and I needed to get home. I decided to sneak out of the party without being noticed and drove myself home. I had no business driving in my drunken state of mind. This time I blacked out and hit something. To this day, I do not know what I hit.

Whatever it was, it took off. I ended up in the hospital with my hip out of place. Apparently, the firemen used the jaws-of-life to get me out of my vehicle. Second Warning: Now I have a plate and three screws in my hip.

In 2002, my friends and I were bored. so we decided to grab some alcohol and went to the mountains to play in the snow. We took a rubber raft with us to slide down the side of the mountain. Close to the bottom of the mountain there was a tree. Our plan was to jump out of the raft before we hit the tree. Obviously, this was not a good idea, but alcohol clouded our intelligence.

It was a two-person raft and as we slid down the mountain my friend jumped out; I lost my balance and fell inside the raft. I looked up to see where I was and SMACK! I hit the tree. I was air-lifted in a helicopter to the hospital. I'm lucky I didn't kill myself. Third Warning: I almost break my neck and had to wear a neck brace for several months.

Three warnings and three collisions due to drinking alcohol clouding my judgement. One plate, three screws, jaws-of-life, and a helicopter ride later I still felt like I had control over this alcohol demon inside of me.

In 2004, I went to a bar to have some drinks with a girl that I was interested in knowing better. I drove her home and headed back to my place, but I got pulled over by the police. Fourth Warning: I received my second DUI.

Pissed-off over the hoops I had to jump through to get my life back in order, I decided to get drunk. Just two weeks after my second DUI, I was drinking and driving and got pulled over again. Fifth Warning: I received a third DUI.

OK, I had had enough. This was getting stupid! I lost my driver's license once again, only this time for three years. I was fined and did one-hundred-eighty days of work release instead of going to jail. I also had one and a half years of DUI classes to take. During this process of my screwed-up life, I met a woman who would help me get sober. Sure enough, I stopped drinking for the three years that my driving privileges were taken from me. My life got better. I paid my fines, finished the one-hundred-eighty days of work release, finished the year and a half of DUI classes, and got my driver's license back.

I was doing really well: professionally, financially, and with my sobriety. I am a store manager at a grocery store making good money with full benefits and a bright future. Then it happened. The woman that helped me stop drinking and I, split up. I started drinking again, only this time with a vengeance. No matter the length of time you stop drinking, you pick up where you left off.

Now I was drinking every day. Also, the more money you earn, the more money you spend on things you think you need. I felt like I needed alcohol. I didn't feel normal without drinking alcohol and thought I could control it.

December 21, 2009, my best friend and I had the day off and we decided to go to a bar to have some drinks and a good time. When you drink alcohol and get behind the wheel of a vehicle, you don't think about the danger you are about to put yourself and everyone else around you in. We are driving home and I blackout again, only this time there are no more warnings and I injured more than just myself. I ran through a stoplight and hit a diesel truck that was making a left turn. For the second time, firefighters used the jaws-of-life to get me out of a vehicle, and for the second time I took another helicopter ride to the hospital. I had four cracked ribs, a punctured lung, and a split-open scalp. But, that was not the worst part; my best friend was DEAD! Why couldn't I heed the warnings?

> In 2015, 91% of people killed in alcohol-impaired driving crashes were one of the drivers or passengers.
>
> *NHTSA National Center for Statistics and Analysis*

Words cannot explain how awful I feel. I have to live with this guilt for the rest of my life. Not a day goes by that I don't think about all the pain and suffering I caused by choosing to drink and drive. Nothing I can say or do can change what I did. The only thing I can hope for is that my life story will open the eyes of someone who may be headed down the same path that my life took and inspire him/her to change direction.

As for me, I will not allow alcohol in my life ever again. If you're going to drink, make sure that you don't have access to any car keys and make arrangements ahead of time to get home safely. Don't give alcohol a chance to ruin your life or those you love. Alcohol causes the brain to formulate the common misperception that one is capable of driving, one can handle anything, and that one can get behind the wheel and drive safely.

Alcohol is a demon that you cannot control behind the wheel of a vehicle. It impairs your judgement and slows down your reflexes. You may get away with drinking and driving for a time, but eventually something will happen that will stop you from doing it again. Hopefully, it will only be a DUI and not an auto collision that ends someone's life.

    The worst mistake of my whole life was to drink and drive. If you are in a DUI class listening to or reading this testimonial, heed my warning and please don't end up like me. My name is Dave, I am serving a life sentence for drinking and driving, and my best friend is DEAD because of it!

IN HIS OWN WORDS
Michael

It was a bright sunny day and pay day. I had worked overtime for several days, so I was sure to have a big check at the end of the week; just in time for my daughter's birthday. She would be turning four years old, and I knew she'd love a children's motorized car.

Once at work my day seemed to be dragging on until my buddy Robert came over to my area with a nice cold beer. I could always count on Robert to come through. We'd both be fired on the spot if the boss knew we were drinking, but what's the big deal? It's Friday and a slow day. I worked hard enough for this little enjoyment. Besides, Robert and I knew how to be discrete. We discretely drank on the job at least three times a week. Before long Robert and I had knocked back a six-pack of beer. I was feeling just right.

I got off work and drove to my favorite check-cashing spot. It's my favorite spot because the liquor store was next door. My drinking wasn't a problem. The only problem was other people trying to tell me what's good for me. If drinking is so bad, why would it be legal? Once my check was cashed I stopped to buy a six-pack of beer, a pint of whiskey, one of those magazines my old lady love's to read and some candy for my daughter.

I arrived home and everyone was happy to see me especially because I brought candy for my daughter and a magazine for my wife. I told my daughter to get ready to go the toy store. I wanted to buy something special for her. She lit up with excitement and quickly got ready to go. After I drank one more beer and downed a couple shots of whiskey, we left the house; just my little princess and I.

She hopped into the front seat of the car like a big girl and I tightened her seat belt. My wife stood on the porch and waved to us as we drove off. We drove to the end of the block and just as I started to make a right turn, BAMM!

When I woke up it seemed like hours had past, but it only had been a few seconds. I looked over and my daughter was crying with broken glass all over her. My princess was bleeding from her head. The

> Nationwide, more than one-quarter (28%) of the total fatalities were in alcohol-impaired driving crashes.
>
> NHTSA May 2018

other driver was lying motionless hanging halfway out of his car. My wife opened the passenger door and pulled my daughter out of our mangled car. She was crying and yelling at me, "What have you done?"

Before I could say anything, it dawned on me that I'd been drinking. Up until that moment, I had not even considered it a problem to drink and drive. It wasn't even on my radar as a problem, threat or issue. It wasn't long before the police, ambulance and a crowd gathered. They rushed to treat the guy in the other car and then came to my princess and I.

The other driver had open liquor bottles in his car and was in really bad shape. Another driver described to the cops the erratic nature of the other man's driving right before the crash. Like a coward, I remained silent and tried to comfort my daughter. We went to the hospital to be sure that we were fine. The other guy was in intensive care for several weeks. He ended up appearing in court for a driving under the influence (DUI) ticket; subsequently, he was sent to a DUI class. This wasn't his first offense. Fortunately, no one died.

I realized that I was the other drunk driver that day. I could have killed my princess and the other driver. I could have avoided that crash had I not been drinking. I held a distorted perception of alcohol and its role in my life. Even my wife didn't view drinking as an issue until that fateful day. My princess didn't get her motorized car that year. Instead, my car was totaled, and we weren't in a position financially to buy another car, let alone extra items.

To anyone who thinks driving drunk or even buzzed is a joke, think of your child, think of your best friend's child, think of yourself. Our ability to operate effectively is severely impaired when we drink. For me, I had a deeper issue that needed to be addressed: I was an alcoholic who needed treatment. My ignorance of placing my child, others and myself in danger was a clear sign of the insanity of my addiction.

Learn from my errors. I won't say mistake because to get

into a car after drinking is a bad choice. It was a series of bad choices, not mistakes. I needed to make different choices. Today, I make better choices and have been sober one-day-at-a-time for sixteen years, seven months and eleven days.

My daughter is now a full-grown woman and a mother herself because I chose not to drink and drive again. That day I could have ended her birthdays. I owe my sobriety to her and every citizen.

This is my story. *Listen,* learn and change.

IN HIS OWN WORDS
David T.

My name is Dave, and I am twenty-eight years into a prison sentence of forty-eight years to life for the murders of Lisa, Ann and Greg, and causing injury to Terry while driving under the influence of alcohol (DUI). I was twenty-three years old at the time the murders happened, and I already had three prior DUI convictions.

Growing up I had a good childhood raised by caring parents and with a religious upbringing. I had two brothers and two sisters and grew up in Northern California. I had many friends in my neighborhood. I did well in elementary and junior high school, getting good grades and excelling in sports. But, all was not well.

Adolescence was a difficult time for me. Like many boys in their early teens, I was interested in girls but felt awkward around them and didn't know how to act. Added to my insecurities, I was a late bloomer. Most of my friends were changing with puberty, but I was not. They were growing taller and more muscular; they were growing hair in places where I was not. Most troubling to me was that I felt like a boy trying to compete with men in sports.

At the age of thirteen, many of my peers started to experiment with drugs and alcohol. It was the late seventies and I also became curious about drugs and alcohol. One day after school, I was at a friend's house and his parents were not home. He suggested that we raid his parent's liquor cabinet and I agreed. It tasted awful and at first, I could not understand why anyone would drink this stuff. Then a magical thing happened.

I started to feel a little dizzy.

> Underage drinking is a serious public health problem in the United States. Alcohol is the most widely used substance of abuse among America's youth, and drinking by young people poses enormous health and safety risks.
>
> NIH, National Institute on Alcohol Abuse and Alcoholism

I also felt very good. We saw a couple of girls from school walking by and we started talking to them. I realized that I didn't feel awkward. The first time I experienced alcohol's affects happened to be the same day that I first kissed a girl. Alcohol became my new best friend, but I didn't realize how much control it had over me.

From that day forward, I felt the need to use alcohol at every social activity where there would be members of the opposite sex. School or church dances, sports events, or cruising the shopping malls all necessitated drinking alcohol. In the beginning, there seemed to be no negative consequences to my drinking. I definitely had to hide this behavior from my parents, especially because they didn't drink. Abstinence from alcohol was part of my religious upbringing. I need to note that soon after I started drinking alcohol I was also experimenting with other drugs.

About a year after I started this new direction in life, my parents became suspicious about my activities outside the home. They heard comments from other people and confronted me, but I denied everything. It wouldn't be long before I couldn't hide it anymore.

At the age of sixteen, I experienced my first blackout. It was a school day and I was in my junior year of high school. I had acquired a large bottle of vodka, mixed it with some orange juice and kept it in a bottle that I took to school. It was a strong mix and I was drinking from the bottle throughout the morning. I was already feeling quite drunk after school, but went home and retrieved my bottle of vodka and continued to drink well into the evening with a friend of mine. Around five or six o'clock in the evening I had no memory of what happened, but I continued to drink. My behavior became more and more erratic and I had to be watched by friends of mine.

I hadn't been home for dinner. This was a problem for my parents because they were concerned about me. I don't know how I got home or at what time. I know I tried to sneak into the house through the backyard, by way of the kitchen and up to my room, but my parents were awake and confronted me. My mother was very angry with me and couldn't understand why I was drinking alcohol. She didn't know that I was coming out of a blackout, was confused and still very drunk. I just wanted to go to bed and sleep, but mom wanted answers that I was not capable of giving her at that time.

She persisted, and I became extremely angry and then violent. I grabbed a knife and threatened to kill my parents. They retreated to their bedroom and called the police. During the time it took for the police to arrive, I was screaming and ranting like a lunatic and acting suicidal. When the police arrived, they tackled me to the ground and I vaguely remember begging them to just kill me and put me out of my misery. That night I was taken to the hospital in a straitjacket.

When I recovered from the excessive alcohol consumption and began to realize what happened, I was horrified at what I had done. I could not believe that drinking alcohol would cause me to be violent. I had never heard of blackouts and I thought it meant to be passed out. Yes, I quit drinking for a little while, but that didn't last long.

Even though I was sixteen years old, I had not earned my driver's license. This did not stop me from driving though. I felt like going for a drive one night after drinking with my buddies. I found a spare key to my dad's car, and sneaked past my parent's bedroom and into mine. I then sneaked out my window and quietly pushed the car away from the house before I started it up. Being young, dumb and drunk, I wasn't obeying the rules of the road and was pulled over and arrested. I don't remember all the charges, but what it meant for me was that I wouldn't be able to get my driver's license until I turned eighteen. That was my first DUI.

Near the end of my senior year in high school, my drinking became progressively worse. I was cutting school often and consequently my grades were suffering. I was more interested in getting drunk, high and chasing girls. When I found out I wouldn't be able to graduate with my class because of poor grades, my parents had enough. They came to me with an ultimatum: go into drug and alcohol rehab or move out of the house and try to make it on my own. I didn't have a job and I knew I wasn't capable of taking care of myself. I knew the alcohol and other drugs were causing a lot of the problems and would continue to do so, if I didn't do something different. I chose rehab.

At first, I thought I'd go to this thirty day program and I'd be cured. I soon learned there is no cure for alcoholism. I would have to treat the disease of alcoholism for the rest of my life. Treatment included attending Alcoholics Anonymous (A.A.) meetings, getting a sponsor and following the Twelve-

Steps that are suggested as a program of recovery. This was a lot to digest as an eighteen year old kid. To make matters worse, when I attended my first A.A. meeting, they started talking about God. I wasn't there to join a new religion. I didn't understand how all this was supposed to fix me and it seemed to be way too much work. I was angry that everybody expected me to understand alcoholism and to figure out the process of recovery.

The counselors at the treatment center realized I didn't take things seriously. They suggested to my parents that further treatment would be necessary if I was to have any hope of recovery. They also suggested an out-of-state facility in Minnesota. I was furious. It took me a week to calm down. When I realized my fate was sealed, I had my first lesson in what it meant to surrender. I decided that I was going to try and make the best of this new situation. The experience was tough but rewarding. The instructions geared toward younger people helped me accept the lessons and teachings a lot easier. I met a lot of great people from all over the country, and I learned some things about myself.

After treatment, I went to a halfway house for ninety days. This was my transition to going home. Counseling was available and A.A. meetings were mandatory. With the A.A. and other programs, I learned about alcoholism and myself. I still had reservations in the back of my mind. I was convinced I wasn't going to drink or use drugs ever again. I didn't believe I needed to go to A.A. meetings regularly, or even get a sponsor. This was my downfall.

When I finished my program at the halfway house, I was allowed to return to my parent's home. I took the classes I needed to earn my high school diploma and I started working as a draftsman for my father who owned an architectural firm. I went to a few A.A. meetings and reconnected with some people I had met in rehab, but I never really took recovery seriously. I ended up spending more and more time with friends in my neighborhood who I had known since pre-school. Plus, I never got a sponsor.

One day while at work, I called a neighborhood buddy to see what he would be doing later. He told me that he and a few other friends were going to a concert and tickets were still available. I decided to go with them and that I'd be the designated driver since I didn't drink or use drugs. When we got to the concert, one of my friends had some pot and started passing around the pipe. You could not have convinced me earlier that evening that I would ever use drugs again, but a thought suddenly came to my mind that I could try an experiment to see if I was really an addict. It happened just that fast.

Nothing bad happened that evening, or so I thought. I wasn't craving getting high the next day or even the day after that. But, addiction is cunning, baffling, and powerful. The fact that nothing bad happened while at the rehab center made me think the counselors were wrong. I was young and dumb then. Now I had grown up. I could handle it now. That was four months out of rehab.

Within six months after first using marijuana and alcohol again, I was binge drinking and having blackouts. I was no longer working for my dad; office work was not for me. I was driving a forklift in a warehouse for a chemical company. I was still living with my parents and it wasn't long before they knew I was drinking again. My poor parents, they didn't know what to do. They didn't want me in the house anymore, but they were not ready to give up on me either.

My dad knew I liked to work with my hands. In fact, in high school I loved woodshop so much that I thought I would be a cabinetmaker when I graduated. Now, I had a new interest, cars. One day my dad talked to me and asked if I had ever considered going to a technical school to learn auto mechanics. I said no, but I liked the idea. He had already checked out the school and had all the details. Dad knew me better than I knew myself.

I moved out of my parent's house, so I could be close to the school. To help offset my expenses, my dad helped with the rent and I had two roommates. Now, my drinking went unchecked. My roommates were almost as bad as me when it came to drinking and irresponsible living. I got my second DUI soon after I started school. I kept my driver's license by taking a DUI class and paying a large fine.

Even though my grades were good in school, I almost didn't graduate because of my frequent absences. I convinced my parents to let me move back into their house temporarily until I became employed and saved some money to move out. They agreed. Then I got my third DUI. I was able to get a provisional driver's license that allowed me to drive to another DUI class, and to and from work only. I quit the class; consequently, the Department of Motor Vehicle (DMV) took my license away. Nevertheless, I continued to drive and drink.

I moved out of my parent's house after I had found a decent job at a tune-up and smog shop. They were not aware that I didn't have a driver's license. Somehow I managed to be reasonably dependable at the shop even though every night was a party that lasted into the wee hours. I became accustomed to working with a hangover. My girlfriend of three years came from a family of drinkers and was now putting pressure on me to lighten up on the drinking. I broke up with her because I wasn't willing to cut back on my drinking. The reality was I needed to stop drinking but I could not. At least not by myself.

Although I was hired for jobs, I couldn't keep them due to my drinking. I continued to drink and use drugs heavily and drive drunk without a license or insurance. I was going downhill fast. I made some sorry attempts at quitting and even attended a few A.A. meetings, but I'd watch the clock instead of listening to the speakers knowing I was going to the liquor store or to meet my connection afterwards.

Everything changed on that November night in 1988. I had an argument with my girlfriend, which was my way of opening the door to a night of unrestricted heavy drinking. I went to a buddy's house and drank about a six-pack of beer. He said he had to work in the morning and called it a night. I drove to a liquor store, bought a half pint of rum, a cola and drove to another friend's place. I continued to drink there and blacked out. When I came out of the blackout, I was in intense pain and someone was stitching up a deep cut on the bridge of my nose. I was confused. I had no idea what had happened. At first, I thought maybe there had been an earthquake or perhaps a natural gas explosion. My whole body hurt, and my last memory had been at my friend's place, so I assumed my injuries occurred there.

Then, I realized I was in a hospital and medical people were around me. I asked what happened and they were astonished that I couldn't remember. Apparently, they told me earlier, but I was still in a blackout. They explained that I had been driving and I hit another car. One person was dead, and two others probably wouldn't survive. It is difficult to explain everything I felt in that moment. A terrible wave of shame overcame me. I wanted to disappear and not exist anymore. I hoped I was dreaming but I knew I wasn't. I uttered my first honest and earnest prayer ever, "God, I can't do this by myself." My life changed forever.

At my arraignment, the charges of Gross Vehicular Manslaughter were raised to Second Degree Murder because I had prior DUIs and attended DUI classes that had warned me of the dangers of driving drunk. Malice was implied because I continued to drive drunk and consciously disregarded human life. I knew drinking and driving was potentially deadly, but I did it anyway. I was tried and convicted of three counts of Second Degree Murder and one count of causing injury while driving under the influence.

The prosecutor explained during sentencing that I had been given every opportunity society could provide. Parents who cared about me, did everything they could and a judicial system that cut me slack on numerous occasions. I had never obeyed the conditions of probation. What choice did the court have? Why should they show me any sort of leniency? The judge agreed and sentenced me to forty-eight years to life in prison.

For a long-time I felt this sentence was unfair. I appealed the decision and lost. Over the years I have come to understand the court's decision. I have been in recovery now for almost twenty-eight years and part of A.A.'s Twelve-Step program involves self-examination. Living these Twelve-Steps daily, I have now come to agree with the court. I needed to be removed from society because I was a danger. I refused to deal with my addiction, so lives were lost and damaged. My actions required a price to be paid. I cannot undo what I did. That said, I changed the person I was with the help of my growing faith in God and A.A.

The prayer I said on the hospital table was answered. From that time forward, my obsession with alcohol was removed. To me that is nothing short of a miracle, but I still have to do the work. Alcoholism cannot be cured, but I can recover with lifelong treatment. Yes, I am in prison, but today I am able to treat my illness with regular attendance in A.A. and by following the Twelve-Steps. They work, but only if I take it seriously. It is my hope that you who read my story and identify with all or part of it will seek help.

IN HER OWN WORDS
Nancy, Alcoholics Anonymous (A.A.) Sponsor

I never had just one or two drinks. All I could think about was, "After I finish this one where will I get my next one?" What I've come to realize, one drink is too many and a thousand aren't enough. Alcohol made me feel about myself all the good things I couldn't be on my own – more likeable, smarter, prettier, and on and on. I had totaled one car while drinking but didn't lose my license or even get a DUI, unlike today. I think the cops just didn't want to deal with it. I managed to drive my next car off a small cliff into a construction zone while in a blackout and totaled the front end. Good-bye car number two. I had to appear in court, but while I was in the bathroom, my name was called, and I missed my chance to go before the judge. Upon leaving the bathroom, a young nice lawyer offered to help me, and the case was dismissed.

One time while very drunk I was driving through the night and into the next day to an outdoor rock concert when I hit a black cat. I knew right away I had done it but kept on driving. The guy I was with even asked me, "Didn't you see you just hit a cat?" and I flat out lied about it. Behind the wheel I was a mess. How it came to pass that I didn't hit and kill anyone in a car while driving drunk is just dumb luck. I escaped horrible car wrecks and automobile tragedies, but I paid a terrible price emotionally.

During the last few months of my drinking I tried to control it. I knew that it was getting out of hand. I tried to tell myself that I would come home early to have a glass of milk first to coat my stomach, or not to switch between beer, wine or hard alcohol. But none of that worked, and I eventually hit a bottom with my drinking. A very public bottom.

I went away for the weekend with my boyfriend with whom I had a big fight. He hit me in front of everyone. It was a really bad scene. The next morning when he dropped me off

> More than half of all adults have a family history of alcoholism or problem drinking, and more than 7 million children live in a household where at least one parent is dependent on or has abused alcohol.
>
> *National Council on Alcoholism and Drug Dependence*

at my house it finally occurred to me that had I not been so drunk none of that would have happened. It was a beautiful sunny Sunday morning and I looked up at the sky as if God was beaming down on me. The reality that I had a drinking problem was undeniable. I suddenly knew that I had to get help. My father had been an alcoholic and died from this disease at the age of forty-three, so I knew where my drinking would ultimately take me.

A few days later when I felt physically better, I drove myself to an Alcoholics Anonymous (A.A.) meeting in the next town. I was too ashamed to attend a meeting in my own town for fear that someone I knew might recognize me. It was three weeks before my twenty-first birthday when I would have been legal to drink alcohol. But God had better plans for me. Some thirty-seven years later I'm still in A.A. and wouldn't trade one day of it for any alcohol. Alcoholism is cunning, baffling and powerful, so I continue to go to meetings to be reminded of this fact. This is a disease that tries to tell me I don't have a disease and it wants me dead. It may have killed my father but by living one-day-at-a-time, it hopefully won't kill me. Today, I have peace and serenity and no longer feel like my life is out of control or that I have no choices. I am happy, joyous and free and live the life I want to live.

A.A., while it has no formal rules, has lots of good suggestions for what works to stay sober. One suggestion is to get a sponsor. A sponsor is someone to walk you through the Twelve-Steps of Alcoholics Anonymous program. It's someone you can confide in and talk freely. You and your sponsor meet as equals. One alcoholic helping another. Men pick male sponsors and women pick female sponsors. Alcoholism is a lonely disease, so keeping in close contact with someone who understands what you're going through is comforting and eases the recovery process tremendously. Not many of us could ever stay sober on our own. I have sponsored many women over the years. It has been such a blessing as they have helped me to stay sober. Like the saying goes, "You lose it if you don't give it away."

For most of us alcoholics, we've come from a long hard road of emotional, physical, financial and spiritual wreckage. We come from all socioeconomic and cultural backgrounds. Some of us have lost everything from our spouses, homes and jobs while others have been able to see early on where they were headed and avoided such loss. Alcoholism doesn't discriminate by any means. While we may have caused tremendous hardship on ourselves and others, especially loved ones, we can stop if we don't take the first drink. What I have learned in A.A. is that it's the first drink that gets you drunk and not the fifth, eighth or even fifteenth. Looking back, I don't think I ever had just one drink.

Perhaps the scariest part of my drinking episodes were the blackouts: the times when I would wake up the next day and not remember anything that had happened hours earlier. I drove in blackouts, talked with people in blackouts and could not recall any of it. How embarrassing it is when friends tell you what you said and did the night before. I've known people who have driven in blackouts and killed people and don't remember a thing. I've heard other women's stories of when they were getting married or giving birth to their child in a blackout. How sad it is for them not to remember those events. Parts of the brain chemistry have been affected and these memories are gone forever. Blackouts are a sure and definite sign that you have a problem with alcohol and need to get immediate help.

The most important key to staying sober is to build a spiritual life. I grew up in the church that my family attended, but it had no personal meaning to me and was rife with religious legalism. A.A. is not a religious program, it is a spiritual one. I learned that something greater than myself keeps me sober. On my own, my life is a mess. But with the grace and love of a *Higher Power*, I am happy, joyous and free today.

Many of us could go for long periods without alcohol, but ultimately when we began to drink again, we couldn't stop. I wasn't in trouble every time I drank, but when I was in trouble, I was always drunk. Do you plan events in your life around the next drink or party? Can't wait until happy hour starts or until you get home where you can safely *tie one on?* Do you get angry or frustrated when the bottles you were hiding are now empty or have been discovered? Normal people don't do these things. Does alcohol make you feel smarter, braver, prettier or more outgoing? There is a solution. It is the program Alcoholics Anonymous.

Once you have started drinking, your brain starts to lose its cognitive abilities of reason, judgment, memory, and spatial perception. The last thing anyone should do after drinking alcohol is get behind the wheel of a car, motorcycle, boat, machinery or anything that can be so deadly. It is a sure ticket to tragedy. Trust me, as one who attends A.A. meetings regularly and is a sponsor, many of us in recovery have our share of regrets.

One of the most poignant things I ever heard early on in my sobriety was the quote from Otto Von Bismark, "A good man learns from his mistakes, a better one learns from the mistakes of others." Live and learn from my mistakes and don't make the same ones. It will save your life and very possibly the lives of others.

A.A. PREAMBLE ©

Alcoholics Anonymous is a fellowship of men and women who share their experience, strength and hope with each other that they may solve their common problem and help others to recover from alcoholism. The only requirement for membership is a desire to stop drinking. There are no dues or fees for A.A. membership; we are self-supporting through our own contributions. A.A. is not allied with any sect, denomination, politics, organization or institution; does not wish to engage in any controversy, neither endorses nor opposes any causes. Our primary purpose is to stay sober and help other alcoholics to achieve sobriety.

The A.A. Preamble is reprinted with permission of the A.A. Grapevine, Inc.

IN HIS OWN WORDS

My name is Jim. I grew up with my mom in a middle-class home in California feeling loved and safe. I enjoyed my childhood. As a teenager I found work as a carpet installer, which became my career. The money was good, but instead of saving or planning for the future, I started hanging out with people who drank alcohol, smoked weed, and used speed. What attracted me to this crowd was the acceptance, the fun, and the idea of living loose and carefree. I knew the drugs were illegal, but I didn't think of myself as a criminal. I worked hard, and I liked to party. Driving while intoxicated didn't seem like a crime to me.

When I was twenty-one years old, I got arrested for driving under the influence (DUI). I viewed it as nothing more than an expensive traffic ticket. Then, I met someone who explained how I could make easy money forging checks, so I tried it. I got arrested and sentenced to sixty days in the county jail. Those sixty days were enough for me. I decided to stay away from that criminal activity, but I continued hanging out with the party crowd and living without a long-term purpose.

For the next ten years I worked and partied. Although I knew I should be more serious about what I could do with my life, I didn't want to pull away from my friends who were part of the party crowd. I had no goals, except to have fun after work and on the weekends.

One summer day in 2000, I was drinking tequila with a friend at a casino. Actually, I didn't drink much that day, and only felt slightly buzzed. I was not drunk! Early afternoon we climbed

Arizona Department of Transportation

into my truck, left the casino and returned to our home area. We hadn't traveled very far when I tried to pass a car on the right. I swung out too far and my right tires went into a sandy rut. I struggle to remember everything from that point on, but my truck spun out of control and lurched across the road crashing head-on into an oncoming car with a woman named Joan and her eleven year old son. Joan died instantly, while her son was injured. My passenger and I were thrown out of the truck as it flipped on the road. The truck crashed into a second car, injuring two other women.

After the crash, I was still conscious, but confused. I stood up in the road and was nearly hit by an oncoming car. I remember being loaded into an ambulance. The next thing I remember was waking up in a hospital trying to understand where I was and why I had an IV in my arm. I saw my mother and father near my bed. They left the room and a police officer began talking with me. He told me that I had murdered an innocent woman and that I would have many years in prison to think about what happened.

I was convicted of Second Degree Murder and sentenced to prison for thirty-four years to life. Although my alcohol level was below the legal limit, my judgment was impaired, and I could not claim that *it was just an accident*. Driving while buzzed is a crime. It showed how insensitive I was to the safety and welfare of others. I have now been in prison for sixteen years.

When I got into my truck that day and drove away from the casino, I could not have imagined that within a few minutes I would kill an innocent mother and devastate multiple families, including my own. My attitude was, "I just want to have a good time." I felt it was no one else's business if I wanted to drink and drive. But, it became other people's business when my careless attitude about the safety of others resulted in death and destruction. The results are beyond what I could have ever imagined.

IN HIS OWN WORDS
Peter W.

My name is Peter, and I grew up in a beach town in California. Until I was forty-five years old, I had a great life by the ocean; in the beautiful redwood forests of the mountains where I went to high school. I had a close loving family. My life centered around the ocean. I loved beach combing and collecting seashells and driftwood with which I made hanging mobiles and other forms of art. I enjoyed free-diving and was certified in scuba diving in 1968. I loved spearfishing, abalone diving and every kind of ocean fishing including deep sea fishing, from a boat in the kelp beds offshore, from the piers, the cliffs, the rocks and the beach.

My family also loved crabbing in the kelp beds while we fished. My biggest passions were surfing, playing harmonica and tending our garden. We also loved camping and bass and steelhead fishing in the Sierras. Vacations in Mexico included surfing, fishing, scuba diving, sightseeing and enjoying the culture and cuisine of the Mexican people. I also loved to party. I loved surfing and partying so much that I turned down an offer to go to an out of state university where my tuition and room and board would be paid for the duration of my schooling. I was short-sighted and regret my decision. I strongly advise people of any age to go to college, it's never too late.

Photo Courtesy of Lorraine Limon Smith

Throughout my life, beginning at eighteen years of age, I drank alcoholic beverages. I began with beer, but soon drank the harder stuff. I accepted drinking as a normal part of my life, my happy go lucky party lifestyle. After all, everyone partied. Now I know I should never have taken that first drink.

I am now a sixty-four year old man full of constant shame and sorrow. My sorrow will be with me for the rest of my life. It began when I was forty-five years old. You see, I murdered an innocent man because of my drinking while driving. I should not have been drinking in the first place because I was severely sleep deprived. Alcohol and sleep deprivation are an extremely dangerous combination, especially when someone is driving.

I murdered a good, kind, hard-working man. A young man with his whole life ahead of him. He was a California Highway Patrolman (CHP). A family man. A valuable asset to our state and one who helped many people in his years of service. I am filled with sorrow, remorse and empathy for what I've done. I plunged his entire family and all of his many friends and co-workers into the horrible nightmare as well.

I think of all the people he met in his life. The people he helped along the way and all those connected to him in various ways – the police, medical personnel, news teams and all those who viewed or read the news. So many people have suffered because of me. To live with this sorrow and guilt is very hard. I can only try to be a better person and try to help others by preventing them from making the same mistake of drinking and driving.

I feel such a strong sense of guilt and shame because I could have and should have prevented this murder. This fine officer would be alive today if I would have had the sense to not drink and drive. There is no excuse to drink any amount of alcohol and drive, or to drive while sleep deprived. The CHP compares driving sleep deprived to drunk driving.

Tragically, it took me forty-five years and the murder to realize the seriousness and danger of this selfish and arrogant crime, driving under the influence (DUI). For years I would drink and drive, and think, "I'm fine, I can make it. I'll just be careful and watch for the police."

Even after receiving four DUIs, I continued to drink and drive. After all I had never been in a car collision. It only takes one! It only takes one auto collision to murder an innocent human being and change the lives of so many people for the worse, forever.

Throughout my life, I received so many warnings from

people about my drinking. I received at least eight drunk in public arrests before I started driving. I've lost jobs. There were days I was too drunk or hungover to surf. I was thrown out of bars, nightclubs, restaurants and parties. I made a fool out of myself at company parties and picnics. I thought that I was the life of many parties when I was actually the fool, the tragic clown. Through the years many family members, friends, strangers, police, lawyers, judges and Alcoholic Anonymous (A.A.) members tried to help me. Why didn't I listen?

That's a question for a psychiatrist to answer. Being diagnosed as bi-polar, I've seen them for forty years. They tried to help me. People said I should not drink because it was poison. It turned me from Dr. Jekyll to Mr. Hyde. So many people warned me of my danger to others and myself. Yet, I did not listen. I thought I knew better, "Heck, everyone drinks."

The last warning I ignored came a week before I murdered this man. It came from a nurse at a local hospital. She told me that if I continued drinking and driving I would kill someone. I shrugged her off saying, "I don't care. I don't care what you have to say. I am here to see my wife, to see how she is doing."

My wife had been in coma with leukemia for a month and a half and in the hospital for two and a half months. I was selfish and arrogant thinking about my life with my wife, over all others. Blind to the danger my actions were to others, to all the warnings, help, breaks and troubles because of my drinking. I thought it was okay to have an eye opener (three fluid ounces of vodka) after work. This drink cost a man his life. This drink ruined his family's life and so many more lives and futures that day because of my drinking and my decision to drink while driving. I murdered a man. I will always feel guilt, sorrow, shame and regret. I will always carry the embarrassment and humiliation of a drunk driving arrest with its jail time, court appearances, fines and public announcement.

A normal, rational person would at least think of drinking less and never driving. Drinking causes so many problems, heartaches and deaths that it is unfathomable that people like me keep drinking and facing those problems time and time again. I learned in A.A. that if a person's alcohol consumption causes continual problems in their life, that they are an alcoholic. Alcoholics who are not in recovery do not think rationally, nor do they think of consequences. They just drink.

I should have learned not to drink, let alone drink and

drive years ago. I should not have started drinking at the age of eighteen. I was attracted to its *feel-good* effects and to the way it masked my shyness, inhibitions and fears; liquid courage.

Alcohol is not the answer. I cannot stress the importance of getting help. If alcohol is causing any problems in your life, get help now. If your life is out of control like mine was, you may be an alcoholic or become one if you drink. It is a progressive illness, and it gets worse! You could actually wake up in a hospital with a police officer telling you how many people you killed.

The point of writing my story is to send a message to each and every one of you. My message – PLEASE, PLEASE do not drink and drive. However sure you are about your ability to drive, if you are under the influence of alcohol, you are not in control. You are lying to yourself. Your thoughts are distorted due to the alcohol. You may get away with driving drunk and reach your destination, once, twice, or maybe for thirty years like me, but it will catch up with you.

As you know, time caught up with me. I killed a man and ruined many lives at the same time. I wrote in the beginning about everything I loved about life. I shared it, so that the reader may realize that you too, could lose all that you love if you choose to drink alcohol and drive, *everything*. Understand that I will never see or do those things again, nor do I deserve to either. Forever, I will live with guilt, horror, regret, shame, and sorrow.

Please do not drink and drive. The act is dangerous, selfish, callous and has proven to be fatal time after time. If you think you may be an alcoholic, please seek help to quit drinking. An alcoholic like myself may think he's fine and can drink without trouble for some time but as in my case, tragedy is inevitable.

No human being should die because a selfish, self-centered person decides to drive drunk with no regard for the lives of others. I would not want anyone to feel like my victim's family, friends, co-workers and so many others who felt the effects of my decision to drink and drive. Also, I don't want anyone to experience what my family, friends and, lastly, myself have experienced because of my decision to drink and drive.

I hope and pray the lessons that I've shared about the worst mistake of my life will be applied to your life and that you will not drink and drive. I beseech you, please learn from my mistakes.

IN HIS OWN WORDS
Jonathan B.

In 2003, I killed an innocent woman while driving under the influence (DUI) of alcohol and marijuana. I fled the scene of the collision without rendering aid to either her or her husband. Hours later the police apprehended me several miles down the highway. During my arrest, I told the officers, "It was only an accident...have some sympathy for me."

The way I ended that statement, *for me,* captures the essence of my attitude at that point in my life. Everything was about me; I believed that I was the center of the universe. This selfish perspective affected more than just my decision to drive while intoxicated. It was not until I broke down the different components of impaired driving that I was able to identify the extent of my poor decision-making.

Impaired driving is comprised of two distinct components: 1) the decision to use/drink mind-altering substances and 2) the decision to drive. First, I decided to use psychoactive substances during my adolescence. Instead of facing social anxiety in a responsible way, I embraced the numbing intoxication of alcohol and marijuana. These substances became my source of artificial courage. I denied the fact that I was dependent on these substances with layers of distorted beliefs. One such belief was my concept of *coolness*. As a teen, I believed it was *cool* to engage in adult activities such as drinking alcohol. I also believed it was *cool* to do things that were considered taboo, like smoking marijuana.

As time went on, I chose to associate with people who fit into my perspective of *coolness* and I desperately sought their acceptance. I also held the belief that using drugs and drinking alcohol were effective coping mechanisms. I believed that alcohol and drugs relieved my social anxiety; hence, my self-image improved. In my mind, I would change from a nervous and insecure adolescent into an outgoing, handsome, and exciting man. With tempered nerves, I presumed that my goals of peer acceptance and admiration were achievable. When I was unsuccessful or felt socially rejected, I found solace in the immature thought, "So what, I'm drunk/high."

At the same time, driving recklessly factored into my view of what social acceptance looked like. As a pre-teen, I envisioned a future of freedom – a freedom to go and do whatever I wanted, a freedom that was dependent on obtaining my driver's license. I believed that a driver's license equated to manhood and a thriving social life. It wasn't *cool* to be driven around by one's parents. In addition, I believed *cool* meant being the person who drove everyone around. I believed that it was *cool* to claim to be the fastest driver. I believed driving around town, with my seat lowered and having only one hand on the steering wheel while listening to loud music, was *cool*. Those misguided beliefs led me to believe it was paramount that I obtain both a license and a car. By adopting this frame of mind, I essentially reduced my personal value to a person who owns car.

It was my fear of missing out on something that prompted my habit of driving dangerously. I convinced myself that in order to stay relevant, I had to be at every social function. If there were multiple parties in one night, I would rush from one side of Los Angeles County to the other. To a certain extent, it was a race between loneliness and me. A race in which I refused to slow down or pay attention to the stop signs. I frequently drove recklessly and exceedingly fast while taking numerous shortcuts and disregarding many traffic laws. I needed to make an appearance everywhere to ensure that people did not forget about me or leave me behind.

Anytime the opportunity presented itself, I would get high on marijuana. Since I believed using drugs and alcohol enhanced my social life, it was inevitable that I would decide to drive intoxicated to *the next big thing,* wherever it was located. I told myself ridiculous stories that neither marijuana nor alcohol impaired my motor skills. Therefore, after becoming intoxicated, I often made the poor decision to drive. Most of the time, I would even *hot-box* (driving around while my car filled up with marijuana smoke) on the way to a social gathering. I ignorantly believed it was *cool* to show up some place and have marijuana smoke creep out of my car as I exited. I convinced myself that what was wrong for others did not apply to me, especially driving impaired. I believed that I was above the law. I used this egotistical way of thinking to justify my decision to drive while intoxicated and impaired, thus meeting both the first and second components of a DUI.

When I began attending college, I expanded my substance abuse to include more serious drugs. Although I lived on campus and did not drive often, my mindset to engage in dangerous activities while intoxicated remained. The story I told myself was that the *college experience* necessitated that I adopt a hardcore party lifestyle of womanizing and *getting wasted*. Just like high school, my desire to be accepted surfaced. I resorted to what I believed worked in the past – drinking alcohol and smoking marijuana. I took the party lifestyle even further in college because I believed that the harder I partied, the more social admiration I would gain.

> In 2015, researchers estimated that each year that about 1,825 college students between the ages of 18 and 24 die from alcohol-related unintentional injuries, including motor-vehicle crashes.
>
> National Institute of Alcohol Abuse and Alcoholism December 2015

My decision-making worsened after attending my first college. At that point in my life, I placed a lot of importance on having a car. My social network ranged from Southern to Central California, so my social relations rested on my ability to travel – at least that is what I told myself. With more parties to attend, I began to drive under the influence on an array of illicit substances. By that time, the decision to behave in such a dangerous and careless manner became effortless due to the mindset I had created.

Since I had been driving under the influence of marijuana and alcohol for years, the transition to drive under the influence of other drugs was seamless. Not only did I completely disregard the consequences of my choices, but I also became callous toward the welfare of others. My false sense of invincibility convinced me that the concept of safety did not apply to me. The story I told myself was, "I am an excellent driver, even when I am intoxicated. I would never be a character in one of those tragic DUI stories. I am special." As long as I was able to make the key turn the ignition switch, I was convinced that I was capable of operating a motor vehicle.

I used delusions, justifications, and rationalizations to shape my perspective. The stories I concocted allowed me to remain in complete denial about my irresponsible actions. I simply dispersed the blame when the consequences of my decisions began to manifest because it was easier to divert responsibility. I would erroneously characterize my troubles as freak occurrences. When I was arrested for a drug bust, it was the police informant and my roommate's fault. When I was kicked out of college, it was the Resident Assistant's fault for improperly calling the police. When I clipped a car, it was because I was distracted when something fell off my dashboard. When I drove my car into the center-median, it was because I was overworked and tired. When I was arrested for a DUI, it was simply the result of having an empty stomach. Nothing was ever my fault. Accountability was virtually missing from my life.

Having a blackout was one of my favorite ways to avoid responsibility. I convinced myself that a memory lapse excused any personal accountability, as if the preceding night's events never occurred. When people recounted the previous night's events, I would typically laugh it off and offer a flippant response like, "I was drunk and high." The reality is I am ultimately responsible for everything that occurred during my blackouts because I consciously chose to drink and use. A blackout is not an excuse for anyone's actions.

It took years before I recognized how serious impaired driving was and even longer before I accepted responsibility for my past actions, specifically the murder of the married woman. I hid behind my delusions for several years, especially the one in which I told myself that her death was only an *accident*. The dangers of impaired driving are common knowledge. Before I took her life, I saw countless television commercials, drove past numerous billboards warning against this reckless behavior, and was given multiple admonitions by criminal justice officials. Therefore, I cannot claim that I was unaware of the inherent dangers of impaired driving. Although I pleaded ignorance in the past. I am now keenly aware that my DUI collision was not an *accident*.

In the presence of numerous indicators, I denied the fact that I was a dangerous person. These warning signs were constantly revealing the truth behind my intentions. My incessant decision to use drugs and alcohol was a warning sign. My series of traffic tickets were warning signs. My expulsion from college was a warning sign. My multiple police encounters were warning signs. My frequent blackout episodes were warning signs, and of course, my DUI arrest in May 2003 was the definitive warning sign. Nevertheless, I continued to ignore all those warning signs because I was unwilling to acknowledge that I was too self-centered, shallow, and selfish to own up to the consequences of my decisions. I did not believe that the laws of society applied to me. I was unwilling to face my former reality of immaturity, social anxiety, and addiction. I valued drugs, alcohol, and pleasure-based experiences over my family, my community and my own well-being. I felt it was easier and more convenient to use a *quick fix* such as alcohol and marijuana than it was to deal with life's responsibilities.

No matter what we profess, our actions reveal our beliefs. This is why results are the true testament of one's intentions. DUIs do not simply just happen. For most of my life, I claimed that it was not my intention to drive impaired. However, based on my results and an honest reflection of my past belief system, I deliberately drove my car while impaired. The sad truth is that it was only a matter of time before I killed someone. Upon this discovery, the connections between my past decisions and intentions became clear.

In 2003, I took a woman's life. I deprived her from having a future. I robbed her family of a loving wife and mother. I took a professor away from her college community. These reprehensible facts haunt me daily. She deserved much better, as did the thousands of other tragic DUI victims. Far too many people are killed each year in DUI collisions, and for what?

Driving impaired is completely preventable. I chose to drive while intoxicated because I was a self-absorbed individual who thrived off artificial comfort and personal convenience at the expense of others. In the past, I was unwilling to acknowledge that I was the person who killed an innocent woman, the person who callously ran away from a loving husband who was holding his dying wife in his arms.

Today, I recognize I was that person, and I strive to make amends for the damage I have caused every day. I am committed to living a responsible life – one that is centered on others. A life that does not entertain the mentalities of selfishness and irresponsibility or the distorted thinking that impaired driving is okay.

IN HER OWN WORDS
Mother of a Fatal DUI Hit and Run Driver

My son was someone who went to private school, received exceptional grades, and was an altar boy. We went to church every Sunday. He never spent any time in a prison. Those who knew him, loved him. He wouldn't intentionally harm anyone.

THE NIGHT EVERYTHING CHANGED
It was late, quiet and dark as I slept with my dog lying beside my bed. My youngest son was asleep in his room down the hall at the front of the house. I always felt comfortable and safe in my home, but, in a matter of minutes, my world would be turned upside down and nothing could correct it. Something woke me. Through the crack of my bedroom door a light shone directly on me. This got the attention of my dog who then headed toward it. As I opened the bedroom door there was a policeman inside my home with one hand on a flashlight and the other hand on his gun. I realized that law enforcement agents were in my home, and I didn't have a clue on how they were able to enter my home or what they wanted.

No longer feeling in control of my surroundings and feeling very vulnerable and emotionally shaken, I became terrified of what was happening. Between being abruptly awakened and the energy of myself and the others who were in my home, everything seemed like a blur and had me wondering if I was dreaming. I couldn't wake up fast enough in order to focus or grasp what was happening. I went along with whatever was going on around me.

One police officer came to tell me that my son had just committed murder. My thoughts were racing trying to make sense of what he had just said. Were they mistakenly at the wrong house, and what did he mean, my son? I thought they must have the wrong residence. This couldn't be true. But they assured me, yes, they had the right address and that my son was in custody for a hit and run auto collision. Someone lost their life. I was in such a state of shock that it was out of my mind's scope of comprehension, and I was trying to stop my mind from short circuiting.

Before my son's collision, I was very self-righteous about those who broke the law. I knew that I, or my children, would never break any laws or hurt someone. That was how we were raised. I enjoyed serving on jury duty, where I thought I was fair when considering the charges of the accused. That would soon change, and I would have a whole new outlook on life. Everything changed forever; not only for the victim's family, but also for our family.

I became afraid of what I was supposed to do or say in defense of my son. I grappled with the grief that the victim's family must be going through, without ever having gone through it myself. I couldn't imagine; yet, I tried balancing what their loss looked like and what was ahead for my son. This dark night would be the scale that tested my coping skills with personal trauma and my fears of the worst possible outcome that lied ahead.

THE OUTCOME AND JOURNEY

Most of my mental reasoning was in a state of confusion about what exactly was being told to me by the police officers. My mothering instincts were consumed on the state of my son's well-being. How was he being treated and how he was going to deal with what lies ahead? I also thought about the family who had just lost a loved one. Their grief weighed heavy on my heart. I was torn between three personality positions: mother, caring human and self. I was telling myself it would be okay and that I had to stay strong. Was the police intrusion and my son killing someone with his car really happening? I wanted no part of this truth and tried my best to convince myself this was only a nightmare. My son was locked behind bars and I couldn't touch or console him. I was afraid of the future.

I had no idea where to seek help because I didn't realize I needed it. It wasn't until the morning after the auto collision when I finally spoke to a friendly voice, my fiancé whom could hear the anguish in my voice. Immediately recounting the night's episode, he told me that I needed to visit the site where the collision occurred. He hoped it would open my eyes to the gravity of the collision, but not overwhelm me at the same time. Listening and wanting any kind of help, I would do anything. So, after speaking to him I went looking for the site. I was unable to locate it. That probably was a good thing, because I was alone and hurting terribly. I learned from my fiancé that years earlier he was going to marry someone else, but she and her young son were killed by a drunk driver. The shock of my fiancé sharing his experience ran extremely deep. I couldn't believe that my future husband had to relive his tragedy, but on the other side of the circumstances.

For the next several weeks, I imagined hearing motorcycles constantly roaring in my ears. One day when I was sitting on the living room couch oblivious to everything, my fiancé asked how I was doing. In response, I asked, "Why are there so many motorcycles?" Dumbfounded and desperate, he called out to me in an angelic voice, "Come back, come back."

We both knew then I needed some serious help before I had a nervous breakdown. The next week we started the quest to find a therapist to help me process the reality of what happened and to create a strategy to prepare for the future.

TODAY

After years of court proceedings my son was convicted of Second Degree Murder resulting in a fifteen year to life sentence. Due to this tragic event, two lives were changed forever: one forever gone and the other thrown away to the penal system. Parents never imagine that their child would end up living their life in prison, especially because of a bad choice to drive impaired. That choice cost so much.

When something this catastrophic happens, it will humble the most proud and prideful person. It will bring them to their knees. Over the years I have visited my son in several different prisons. I had never been to a jail, prison, or a detention facility prior to the fatal collision. I never wanted to go, nor did I ever expect to see my son live in such unfortunate and dire conditions. My son's incarceration has been and still is a very rough journey, especially as a mother knowing that I have to support my son unconditionally because of the love I have

A Mother's Love

for him.

There is no therapist or drug that can help put you in the place you were before such an incident and then keep you sane. I returned to the higher power within me and let the gift of faith and trust take over. My prayers to God for forgiveness and mercy have helped me tremendously. These things have brought me the comfort and strength to continue. Through prayer and faith, I have been able to come through this dark valley. I hope that some good comes out of this tragedy, and that it is not wasted. And yes, there has been some good.

By sharing about the consequences of my son's choice to drive impaired with friends, family, and people, I have been able to change their attitudes towards DUI. I especially like conversing with young adults about my son's choices to drink and drive, because they have so much to live for, and I would hate to see their lives shattered by the devastating consequences of impaired driving. It leaves a horrific impact on human lives. It is my hope that the reader finds value in my story.

IN HIS OWN WORDS
Paul

My name is Paul, and I would like to share a little about myself. Born into an alcoholic family, I am the second to the youngest of twelve brothers and sisters. It was only a matter of time before I would start drinking. I loved running around the neighborhood with my friends like a normal kid, because it was an escape from seeing my mom and dad's drinking and fighting.

I started drinking when I was thirteen years old. Drinking alcohol would be the way to hide from all the hurt and pain I experienced as I watched my dad fighting with my mom and him breaking the furniture in the house in a fit of rage. I would take beer from the refrigerator after my dad passed out. From that first day, I drank in order to cope with life's problems and my low self-esteem. Before I knew it, I was using alcohol as courage to cope with my emotions. I felt helpless and alone not knowing what to do. I drank so I was able to talk to people. Little did I know, the only people I communicated with were my so called normal friends who supplied the alcohol and drank with me.

Throughout my youth, I watched my dad drink and drive in his vehicles. I came to view this behavior as normal because that's all I knew growing up in an alcoholic family. Even visiting my dad in jail for his driving under the influence (DUI) tickets was normal. He was killed in a DUI collision. I was twenty years old at the time and started drinking regularly for the next seven years. At that point in my life I stayed drunk because I didn't know how to cope with his death.

Then life really hit me. Five years after my father's death, I lost my mom to cirrhosis of the liver. I had been drinking heavily for the last ten years and had received two DUIs. I also had a wife and two sons at this time. I was so deep into my drinking that I didn't care who I hurt. Yes, I was working and making good money, but, I was living a false life. After all, I was not hurting anyone, or so I thought. I was inflicting emotional pain on my wife and sons.

I didn't realize I had a drinking problem until it was too late. The judge sent me to mandated Alcoholics Anonymous (A.A.) meetings. I didn't care or pay attention to them. I just showed up. All along, the judge was trying to tell me that I had a drinking problem and trying to save someone's life. I was a semi-truck driver, paying the bills and giving money to my wife. I thought I was doing the right thing.

The day before Thanksgiving, I started drinking at six o'clock in the morning in order to get over my hangover from drinking the day before. It was now 4:30 in the afternoon, and I had been drinking throughout the day. I was driving from Los Angeles and heading home when I stopped to buy more beer for the rest of the drive home. It never occurred to me that I was hurting anyone by driving impaired; that behavior was my normal routine.

As I waited in traffic on the expressway, I decided to exit and drive the side streets to the garage, where I always parked the truck at the end of the workday. About a half mile after exiting the expressway, I ran through a yellow light at an intersection. I broadsided a car turning left into the intersection and killed the passenger. She was twenty years old. I took her dreams away. I never gave her a chance at life. My victim was headed to her family's house for the holidays.

I was arrested and booked for Second Degree Murder. I fought the sentence in court for two years. I thought I was innocent. I was in such denial. In fact, I told my attorney to request a traffic accident specialist to testify at one of my hearings. I blamed everyone but myself for the crash. I was charged with Second Degree Murder and was sentenced to fifteen years to life in prison. The last time I was a free man was in November 1995 because I chose to drink alcohol and drive. The reason I received the murder charge was because I chose to let alcohol run my life.

Once in prison, I continued to blame everyone else for my mistakes. I have been incarcerated in many California prisons. I started in a Level Four yard where I have seen inmates killed and stabbed for no reason. In my opinion, a fist-fight is no reason for a Commanding Officer (CO) to shoot and kill any human being. I was thirty years old when I was sent to prison, and experienced a high level of fear as I witnessed this *new stuff* going on around me.

I found out that *making pruno* (jailhouse liquor made from fermented fruit) and hanging around negative peers only reinforced the same false belief system that sent me to prison in the first place. In 2006, I finally saw the flickering light turn on and started to look for a change. My pride was the main characteristic that needed to change and be disposed. I put my pride aside and got rid of the many masks I hid behind. That's when I became a mature man and asked for help. I got into a substance abuse program and learned about myself. I then became a peer mentor. In fact, I recently coordinated a peer mentor program here in prison. I have facilitated A.A. groups and anger management sessions. I also completed *Thinking for Change,* a cognitive behavioral treatment program, to name a few of many self-help groups in which I have participated.

In January 2015, I was diagnosed with stage three colon cancer and after I completed chemotherapy I was found suitable for parole in October 2015. I thought my roller coaster ride was over and I would close this chapter of my life's book. Once again, I found myself in a different prison. In December 2015, I was getting out of the shower when a riot broke out. Because I was in the day room (shower) when it happened the COs said I was involved, so I was taken to the Administrative Segregation Unit (ASU). I was supposed to go home in March 2016; that did not happen.

I have been clean and sober for the last ten years. With my new view on life, I help everybody in prison. I don't care about their race. If someone was hungry, I gave them food. If they needed someone to talk to, I would listen. If someone needed help with homework, I would tutor him. Close to parole, I was charged with battery on an inmate. The weapon was a broom. I never swung a broom handle at anyone, but it was my word verses the COs word.

At that point I had served twenty years on a fifteen year

to life sentence and was found suitable for parole. I was not about to do something that would jeopardize my future freedom. Even though I was found not guilty, the Rules Violation Report (RVR) was filed.

In prison, you never know what's going to happen. In January 2017, I received a three-year parole denial and lost my suitability to go home. It's not from being at the wrong place at the wrong time, but because I chose to drive impaired. I have nobody to blame but myself. My attitude and the actions I live by are mine and mine alone. Today I have taken full responsibility and have done everything possible to change my distorted thinking, so I can leave prison and be a productive member of society. I will not be able to go in front of the Board of Prison Hearings (BHP) until January 2020. I hope and pray that I have helped anyone who is willing to *listen.* Don't drink alcohol and drive. Believe me, I am an honest recovering alcoholic who used to sit in these groups and say, "It would never happen to me."

IN HIS OWN WORDS
Daniel

In many ways, my childhood reflects that of other DUI incarcerated men: immigrant, no father figure (he was an alcoholic and drug addict), no friends, bullied, pressured, low self-esteem, and a young addict and alcoholic. Fast forward to the time when I was fifteen years old.

I had stopped going to school. I became totally hooked on crystal meth and hanging out with the wrong crowd. Even though I had known my soon-to-be best friend at the age of twelve, we didn't become best friends until we started to party together. It was about this time that I needed a friend because the older boys started pressuring me to gang-bang. Although I was selling their drugs, I didn't want to become a gang member. My new best friend was instrumental in helping me stay out of the gang lifestyle. His friendship gave me courage. He influenced me not to go down that road of certain trouble.

With that said, as young and naïve adolescents, we were in a hurry to grow up, wanting to be men in the world. So, instead of participating in gang activities, we joined the party crowd. My best friend was tall and had natural charisma with the ladies. He was quite popular. It seemed as if my best friend and I were destined to be *amigos*. When my mom got a new job, we moved to the same apartment complex where he lived. He and I became inseparable. I never had a friend like my best friend. We even worked landscaping together. Unfortunately, our drug lifestyle got in the way. When we lost one job, we found another.

Eventually I fell in love. She was a beautiful girl, and I longed to be with her. She became my whole focus in life, even my best friend took second place to her. My friendship with my best friend was more important than anything, and I never thought a girl could come between us.

Despite working, I had a hard time controlling my meth habit. Back then I wouldn't call it an addiction, because that meant I would have to confess to myself that I was a slave to this drug. In my mind, I worked, functioned daily, and paid my bills, so I felt like I was a responsible adult. I put on a good mask for the world to see. I was living a lie. I refused to face the truth of who and what I was.

When I was seventeen years old, my best friend and I moved to Utah trying to find different lives for ourselves. I was able to move because I'd obtained a fake identification and Social Security card. We wanted to start a new life in a new town. We found jobs at a carwash, even though it didn't pay a good wage. For the first time in our lives, we rented our own apartment and bought a car. Eventually, we quit our jobs and moved back to Southern California; me with my sister, and him with his mom. I returned to the life in the fast lane, selling and using drugs.

I started working at a restaurant. One night my best friend, before he was to pick me up, stopped to buy some weed. When he didn't show up as planned, I knew something happened. I later learned that my dealer showed my friend a new dirt bike that he was selling. My best friend couldn't resist and took it for a test ride. He loved dirt bikes. Unfortunately, he crashed and broke his femur. He was in a coma for five days. He almost died! I felt a deep sense of guilt because I sent him to pick up the weed.

I took care of him a few times after his surgeries, but he had changed. He wasn't the happy-go-lucky guy I knew. My best friend was miserable. He hated being in a wheelchair as his femur was healing slowly. I tried to cheer him up and bring back his zest for life. I brought him whatever he wanted: drugs, girls, fast food and rented movies. We constantly stayed high, but it wasn't the same. Somehow the crash affected our friendship. I tried to make things right. I don't think my best friend blamed me for his crash and becoming crippled, but I certainly blamed myself. I never wanted to hurt my best friend, but I didn't know how to fix what was wrong with him. All we could do was hope that one day he would be able to walk again without crutches. For a time, I distanced myself from my friend, because I didn't know how to heal our friendship. Eventually, I just stayed away.

When I was twenty years old, I received my first driving

under the influence (DUI) ticket. I had been driving from a bar. I didn't think I was drunk. Other times, I had driven blasted and nothing happened. This DUI ticket was a joke to me, because I was not even *buzzed*. I only had two beers. I got pulled over for a broken tail light, not for driving *blasted*. I couldn't believe it when the cop said I was driving impaired and arrested me. I knew that I passed the Field Sobriety Test (FST). In any case, I went to court and paid my fine, but I ignored the whole situation, telling myself it was ridiculous, that DUI was a *silly* law, and that I had placed no one in danger.

I had met my future wife when I was eighteen years old. We got married when I was twenty years old. My girlfriend was pregnant, and I married her despite all my concerns of thinking it was the right thing to do. We had a son. I didn't want to father a child and then abandon my responsibilities like my father had done with his family. Plus, my wife liked my best friend; they got along well. My wife and I rented an apartment as I tried to be a responsible husband, working and paying the bills.

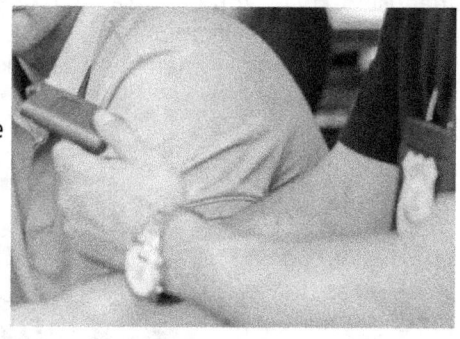

In August 2007, my best friend had the screws in his injured leg removed. It had been a long nine months of not being able to move around. He invited me to watch the UFC Fights. I vowed to make it up to my best friend as the distance that was between us really bothered me, more than I can explain. My friend hated life while being home-bound. He was healed and ready to face the world again, so I bought an eighteen-pack of beer to drink while we watched the fights. My best friend's mom was happy that I was at their house to witness his new-found health and strength. She had known about the rift between us and was anxious for us to be friends, like in days past.

After we polished off the beer, my best friend was roaring to get out of the house. He wanted to go to a nightclub and talked about dancing with the girls. He still had his charisma and could charm the ladies. We laughed at his enthusiasm, but I didn't have a driver's license due to my *silly* DUI ticket. I felt responsible for his condition, and I wanted to do for him whatever he wanted. He wanted to get out and have a grand old time. So, I said, "Screw it," and decided to drive my best friend and his brother to a party. I told myself that I wouldn't drink too much and that my best friend's happiness was more important than my receiving another ticket for breaking the law. We left their house in high spirits, looking to conquer the world and believing nothing could stop us.

At the party, we each had two shots of tequila, then ordered some strong mixed drinks. All thoughts of remaining halfway sober had gone to the wind. We had a wild night and eventually ended up at a bar. My best friend was enjoying his freedom. It was just like the old days; no more distance in our friendship. I was proud to be able to help my best friend have a good time after his injury.

The next thing I remember was waking up in the hospital emergency room with two police officers talking to me. I was out of it and handcuffed to the hospital bed. I passed out again. I woke up as they were putting staples in my knee. The cops were gone by then, but my family was there. I 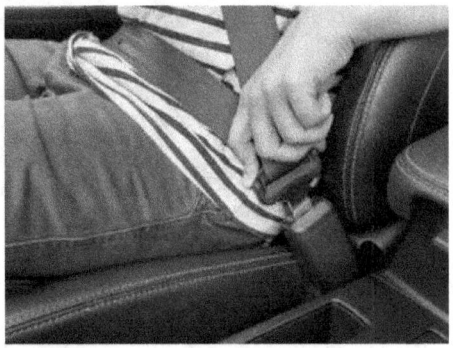 wasn't charged with any crime, so the medical staff let me go. My family took me to the hospital where my best friend and his brother were being treated. By the time I got there, my friend's brother was being released.

He claimed that his seatbelt had saved his life. But my best friend was in a coma after hitting his head during the collision. I was told his brain was swelling and that the medical staff had removed part of his skull to try and ease the pressure. I knew his very life was in the balance. I was numb. I couldn't comprehend that this was happening to my best friend. He was supposed to be dancing, not fighting for his life. It was like a terrible dream that I couldn't wake up from. The hospital staff allowed me to sit on my friend's bed as I held his hand and told him how sorry I was. I was in a daze, a zombie. I cried in his mom's arms and wanted to die. "I don't care about myself," I told her through my tear-filled eyes, "I only want him to be alright." She was crying too and speechless, not knowing what to say.

After a week of my best friend being in a coma, the doctors explained to his mother that he was brain-dead and that there was no hope of him coming out of it. My best friend's mom talked with her family, included me, and then decided to *pull the plug*, taking my best friend off life support. I was heartbroken. I couldn't leave. I never wanted to leave the side of my best friend again, not like I had during his femur recovery. I stayed and watched as they turned off the life support equipment. My best friend was tough, he survived another day without the machines that had previously kept him alive. I kept telling myself that he would magically wake up and that this nightmare would be over. When my best friend died, all my hopes died with him.

The guilt of my best friend's death zapped my will to live. I had no energy for life. I laid in bed day after day, not facing life, not able to face my family, much less my friend's family. They had showed me such love and compassion. How could I ever look his mom in the eyes again, knowing full well what I'd done. I didn't want to live. Five months passed, and then the cops showed up at my door. My wife allowed them to enter not understanding what was happening. I was in bed when they pounced on me and arrested me with a gun to the back of my head.

As they handcuffed me, I remember one of them saying, "Make sure we have the right guy, he has a tattoo on his back." I was completely stunned. They read me my rights explaining I was being charged with Second Degree Murder. I didn't care; they could have shot me right then, and I wouldn't have protested. I killed my best friend. I didn't resist as they escorted me out of my home and into prison for the rest of my life.

From what I understand, the police secured the blood evidence from my hospital stay, and had it tested for intoxication the day of the collision. It was all so crazy. On one hand, I never thought the charges would stick. Didn't they know that the man who died was my best friend? Didn't the courts know that I would have gladly died for him? How could they now say I was a cold-blooded murderer, or that I meant to kill him with implied malice? I was a zombie throughout the entire trial. After I arrived in prison, I turned to heroin to make me numb because I still couldn't face life and what I had done. I was slowly trying to kill myself with the easiest thing I knew - DRUGS!

But, a *LIGHT* entered my life when I discovered a DUI prevention class which gave me a purpose to live. Writing my story is what is keeping me alive and giving me new hope. I have been sober for fifty-nine days at the time of this writing. I now attend classes to understand addiction and how it enslaved me for a lifetime. If I can keep one person from driving intoxicated, I may save an innocent life. I now have a mission to bring awareness to the crime of impaired driving that took my best friend's life and sentenced me to prison.

In the depths of Hell, a concrete cell, I think about my best friend every day. I'm determined to help others from the thoughtless action of driving under the influence. Please think before you drink! Make plans to have a sober driver take you home. Do not think you can have just one drink and all will be well. Don't let my horrific example go to waste. I pray my story makes you do the right thing and not drink alcohol and drive.

In Honor of My Best Friend, DON'T DRINK AND DRIVE!!!

EN SUS PROPIAS PALABRAS
María, Madre Cuyo Hijo fue Asesinado por su Mejor Amigo

Después de recibir una llamada telefónica inesperada de la policía local a las 2 am, llegué al hospital a las 4am y me dirigieron a la habitación donde mi hijo estaba inmóvil. Lo que vi cuando entré en la sala de emergencias todavía me hace llorar cuando comparto mi historia. Mi segundo hijo, que tenía veintidós años, estaba acostado en la cama con la cabeza completamente destrozada. Estaba vomitando sangre debido al trauma en su cabeza. Él estaba irreconocible. Poco después de que lo vi, le llevaro a la sals de cirugía, donde el personal médico le operó durante siete horas.

Después de la cirugía, el médico me informó que pasarían unos cuatro días antes de que se conocieran los resultados de la cirugía. Mi hijo estaba conectado a todo tipo de máquinas y en estado de coma. En el momento del choque, yo trabajaba en el mismo hospital y conocía a muchos del personal médico que estaba cuidando a mi hijo. Ese dia no trabajé, solo pasé la mayor parte de mi tiempo al lado de su cama. El cuarto día, el médico me informó que la condición de mi hijo no había cambiado. El médico explicó mis opciones: mantener a mi hijo con soporte vital y esperar que salga del coma o desconectar a mi hijo de las máquinas de soporte vital.

Mis opciones no fueron buenas. Mantenerlo con vida artificial lo mantendría con vida, pero era muy posible que nunca se despertara del coma. Si se despertaba, lo más probable era que fuera un vegetal por el resto de su vida. Y, podrían pasar de diez a quince años antes, si es que alguna vez, se despertara. Mi otra opción era desconectar a mi hijo de las máquinas y dejar que Dios se saliera con la suya. Elegí la ultima opción, En el quinto día de mi hijo estar en cuidados intensivos, le dije al médico que lo desconectara del soporte vital. Tenía veintidós años y fue la decisión más difícil que tomé. Murió cinco días después del choque a las 5:45 pm en

Agosto de 2007.

Mi hijo era típico joven de veintidós años. Le gustaban las chicas, los videojuegos y la música ranchera Mexicana. Trabajó en el aeropuerto  local como un manejador de equipaje y fielmente me dio dinero para ayudar a mantener a su hermano menor y a mí. El consumo de alcohol también fue parte de su vida, En la noche en que ocurrió el *accidente*, mi hijo, su mejor amigo y otros amigos habían estado bebiendo en un bar local. Cuando salieron del bar a las 2am, mi hijo y su mejor amigo subieron al auto de su amigo y su amigo condujo. Embriagado y presumiendo exceso de velocidad, el mejor amigo se pasó una luz roja y se estrelló contra otro automóvil. Un testigo de la colisión llamó a la policía. Poco después de que llegara la policía, llegó una ambulancia y transportó a mi hijo al hospital.

El mejor amigo y mi hijo habían sido amigos desde la escuela secundaria. La familia del mejor amigo y mi familia vivían en el mismo complejo de apartamentos. Los niños crecieron e hicieron todo juntos. Eran inseparables, y el amigo era como un cuarto hijo para mí. Conozco a su madre desde hace veinte años y hablo con ella regularmente. No tengo malos pensamientos o sentimientos hacia la madre. Hasta el día de hoy, nos invitamos a fiestas. La madre es una buena persona y solo puedo imaginar lo que es tener un hijo en prisión.

El *accidente* ocurrió hace once años. Me refiero a esto como un *accidente* porque nunca tuve mala voluntad o malos pensamientos hacia el mejor amigo o su familia. Fue un incidente desafortunado basado en la mala decisión de que el mejor amigo decidió beber alcohol y conducir, y que mi hijo tomó la decisión de sentarse en el asiento del pasajero, sabiendo que su amigo estaba borracho. Se podría decir que es perdón, pero para mí, no hay nada que perdonar. Ambos muchachos tomaron una mala decisión y nuestras familias sufrieron una pérdida. Mi hijo murió, pero su hijo pasará los próximos quince años a cadena perpetua.

Amo al mejor amigo de mi hijo. Le envío dinero y paquetes

de alimentos en prisión. Quiero ir a visitarlo a la prisión pronto. Su madre me ayudará a completar el papeleo, así puedo visitarlo. Mi hijo más joven fue a visitar al hombre en prisión hace unos tres años. Tengo amor por él, no había nada que perdonar, él es parte de mi familia.

Para aquellas personas que quieren beber alcohol y / o drogarse y conducir, quiero decir que cuando alguien cercano a ti muere, es muy difícil lidiar con su muerte. Si bebe, piense, no beba ni conduzca. Si ha perdido a un ser querido a un conductor discapacitado, perdónelos. Te liberará.

IN HER OWN WORDS
Maria, Mother whose Son was Killed by His Best Friend

After receiving an unexpected, phone call from the local police at 2 am, I arrived at the hospital at 4 am and was directed to the room where my son laid motionless. What I saw when I entered the emergency room still makes me cry when I share my story. My middle son, who was twenty-two years old laid on the bed with his head completely smashed. He was vomiting blood due to the trauma to his head. He was unrecognizable. Shortly after I saw him, he was whisked away to surgery, where the medical staff operated on him for seven hours.

After the surgery, the doctor informed me that it would be about four days before the results of the surgery would be known. My son was hooked up to all kinds of machines and laid in a coma. At the time of the *accident,* I was employed at the same hospital and I knew many of the medical staff that were caring for my son. I did not work but spent most of my time by his bedside. On the fourth day, the doctor informed me that my son's condition had not changed. The doctor explained my options – keep my son on life support and hope that he comes out of the coma or disconnect my son from the life support machines.

My options were not good. Keeping him on life support would keep him alive, but it was very possible he would never wake up from the coma. If he did wake up, he would most likely be a vegetable for the rest of his life. And, it could be ten to fifteen years before, if ever, that he would wake up. My other option was to disconnect my son from the machines and let God have His way. I chose the latter. On my son's fifth day in intensive care, I told the doctor to disconnect him from life support. He was twenty-two years old, and it was the most difficult decision I ever made. He died five days after the *accident* at 5:45 pm in August 2007.

My son was your typical twenty-two year old young man. He liked girls, video games and Mexican Ranchera music. He worked at the local airport as a baggage handler and faithfully gave me money to help support his younger brother and me. Drinking alcohol was also part of his life. On the night the crash occurred, my son, his best friend and other friends had been drinking at a local bar. When they left the bar at 2 am, my son and his best friend got in his friend's car

and his friend drove. Being drunk and showing off by speeding, the best friend ran a red light and crashed into another car. A witness to the collision called the police. Shortly after the police arrived, an ambulance came and transported my son to the hospital.

The best friend and my son had been friends since junior high school. The best friend's family and my family both lived in the same apartment complex. The boys grew up and did everything together. They were inseparable, and the friend was like a fourth son to me. I have known his mother for the past twenty years and I talk to her on a regular basis. I don't have any bad thoughts or feelings toward the mother. To this day, we invite each other to parties. The mother is a good person and I can only imagine what it is like to have a son in prison.

The *accident* happened eleven years ago. I refer to this as an *accident* because I never had ill-will or bad thoughts toward the best friend or his family. It was an unfortunate incident based on the poor decision that the best friend decided to drink alcohol and drive, and that my son made the decision to get in the passenger seat, knowing his *amigo* was drunk. One could say it is forgiveness, but to me, there is nothing to forgive. Both boys made a bad decision and our families both suffered a loss. My son died, but her son will spend the next fifteen years to life in prison.

I love my son's best friend. I send money and care packages of food to him in prison. I want to go visit him in prison soon. His mother will help me complete the paperwork, so I can visit him. My youngest son went to visit the man in prison about three years ago. I have love for him, there was nothing to forgive, he is part of my family.

To those people who want to drink alcohol and/or do drugs and drive, I want to say that when someone close to you dies, it is very hard to cope with their death. If you drink, please think – don't drink and drive. If you have lost a loved one to an impaired driver, forgive them. It will set you free.

IN HIS OWN WORDS
Rudy

My name is Rudy, and I am serving a fifteen year to life sentence for Second Degree Murder. I killed a Police Officer. Needless to say, prison is not what I had planned for my life.

I grew up with my mom as an only child. My dad was an alcoholic and drug addict who would beat my mom and I when he occasionally lived with us. I grew up living in fear and had hatred toward my dad. I was only a kid, but I was ashamed that I could not protect my mom from him. I felt helpless.

By the age of fifteen, I was using drugs with my friends in the neighborhood. I joined a gang. I felt like I belonged. I felt accepted and respected. Soon after joining the gang, I got into trouble with the law for being in possession of stolen property and drugs. Also, my mom kicked me out of the house because I was caught stealing from family and friends. I was twenty-one years old and homeless. That was a wake-up call for me.

I went to rehab and stayed sober for two years. I had a job, a place to live and a car. Life was good. Then, one night I went out with some friends who were drinking. I told myself there was nothing wrong with having a couple of drinks. I told myself that as long as I'm not doing any drugs, I'll be okay. Soon after that evening, I was using drugs again.

I thought nothing of getting behind the wheel and driving drunk or *high*. After all, I had done it countless times before and nothing ever happened. All that changed in September 2005. I had been using drugs for a couple of days and had barely slept. The next morning, I drove to work on drugs and blacked out. Everything after that was a blur. Although I don't remember it, I learned that I plowed my car into an officer as he sat on his motorcycle stopped at a red light. The impact knocked him to the other side of the street, where he landed on the sidewalk unconscious. As I drove through the intersection, still blacked out, a car crashed into me on the driver's side. The crash jolted me conscious, but I still didn't realize I had just run over an on-duty police officer. I was arrested immediately, as I climbed out of my car.

First, I was taken to a hospital to be checked out by medical personnel and then transported to the Sheriff's station. As I rode in the backseat, the sheriff informed me that the officer had died before the paramedics could get him to the hospital. The reality hit me hard when I heard the news. I had just killed an innocent person.

The officer's wife will never see her husband again. His five children will never see their dad again. He was a father, a husband, co-worker, a role model to others and a hero in his community. Because of my criminal carelessness, selfishness, and insensitivity for the safety and welfare of others, a good man who was in the prime of his life, was killed on his way home from work.

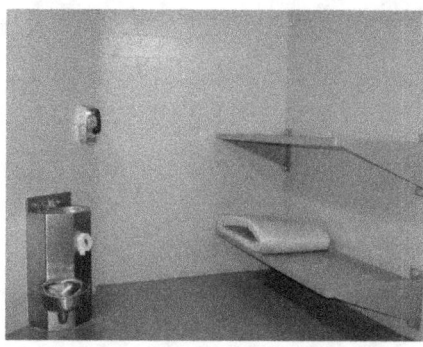

So many lives were severely impacted that day I decided to drive impaired.

At the time, I did not think that getting behind the wheel while being *high* was a big deal. I now realize that every time I drove intoxicated or hungover, I was putting the lives of innocent people at risk. I was a true danger to society every time I drove under the influence.

I have been in prison now for thirteen years with no end in sight because of my life sentence. My days are filled with correctional officers telling me what to do 24/7. I'm locked up in a tiny cell with another man. The cell is only eleven feet long and six feet wide. When one of us uses the toilet, the other one smells it; in addition, we must eat in the same space. There is no getting away from my confinement. No way out. Prison is not a place you would choose to spend even one day, much less the rest of your life.

I wanted to share my story because I know there are many people who don't think or believe this can happen to them. I was one of those people. My action of killing an innocent man was not *bad luck*. It was a result of my repeated reckless behavior, thinking no harm would ever come from it. I will spend the rest of my life in regret for all the families I have harmed. Not to mention my own family, especially my mother. As she advances in years, her only child is not there to help her or to watch over and care for her. I am not there to comfort her with my presence.

I hope you will honor the police officer and his family by thinking of them the next time you consider getting behind the wheel of a car while intoxicated or even hungover.

IN HIS OWN WORDS
Stephen

I never thought it would happen to me, but here I am in a California State Prison serving a life sentence for DUI Second Degree Murder. Before I go into the details of what happened that fateful morning, let me tell you a little bit about myself.

My two brothers and I were raised by two loving parents who provided for us. I am the middle child. My parents are Christians and we went to church regularly. It seemed to me that we lived by stricter house rules than the average kids in the neighborhood. The rules made me feel like I was missing out on sleep-overs at friends' houses, dating girls, and attending rock concerts.

As for school, my grades were above average, but I preferred to play and have fun. I enjoyed baseball, football, tag, hide-and-go-seek, and fishing and hunting at the lake. At the age of thirteen, my older brother and I had the opportunity to attend a Christian summer camp in the mountains for a week. It was a blast playing war and sleeping in tents in the mountains and valleys where we played a game, Capture-the-Flag. On the weekend, church service in the chapel was mandatory. This requirement threw a wet blanket on our fun, because we did not want to attend. At the Friday evening service, my brother, our friends and I, sat in the back pews by the exit door. Sitting in the back enabled us for a quick exit where we could immediately leave and resume playing.

I don't remember listening to a word the preacher spoke, but at the end of the service, he gave an alter call, an invitation to come forward and receive Jesus Christ as Lord and Savior. At that very moment, an invisible force was drawing me to get out of my seat and go forward. I dug my heels in and resisted the force, fearful of what my friends would think if I went up to the front. Although it took all my will and might to do so, I was successful in resisting the unseen force.

The next night, Saturday, the exact scenario happened

again, but this time the force was way too great for me to overcome, so I went up to the front and received the Lord Jesus Christ as my Savior. The moment I did so that drawing, unseen force stopped. The preacher then said, "For those of you who received Jesus Christ as Lord and Savior, there will be a water baptism in the swimming pool tomorrow." Butterflies instantly hit my stomach as I said to myself, "What have I gotten myself into?" Fear struck me at the thought of being baptized in front of the whole camp, but they had my name and knew where to find me. I couldn't get out of it. There was nothing I could do. I got baptized. It turns out to be glorious! I will not go into all the details other than to say, it's all true. I knew in my heart that I was now different inside. I had a spiritual re-birth. I was born-again.

I started my first year in junior high school after that summer vacation. I saw all the cool guys and girls, the *in-crowd;* they were the partyers who smoked tobacco, drank alcohol, used drugs, and had sex. I desperately wanted to fit in and be one of those cool people. However, the Spirit of Christ in me did not want me to do those things. There was a great struggle within me. I eventually pulled away from God. It hurt. I know now that God was right, and I would have been spared from going down the road of destruction that I chose.

At the same time, my older brother, whom I followed everywhere up to that point in life, started on the party road himself. He would not let me hang around him anymore and even pushed me away. He was my idol. I looked up to him and wanted to be like him. He was courageous and would not back down from a fight. When he fought, he won. I did not possess that kind of courage, but I surely wanted it. When my brother pushed me away it really hurt. I decided that I was going to party and be part of the in crowd too. Hence, I started down the road of destruction. At the time, the road looked like it was lined with everything I desired. I tried to hide this new lifestyle from my parents, but of course, I was caught and punished time after time.

One instance, I was caught smoking in the boys' bathroom at school. The principal called my parents. My mom picked me up and once outside of the principal's office, she asked where I got the cigarettes. I gave her an answer she didn't want to hear. So, she pulled me into the car. Once in the car, she asked the same question. I gave her a smart answer and she slapped me across the face, hard! This happened during the break while the students walked to their next class. My new party friends saw the whole thing. I was humiliated.

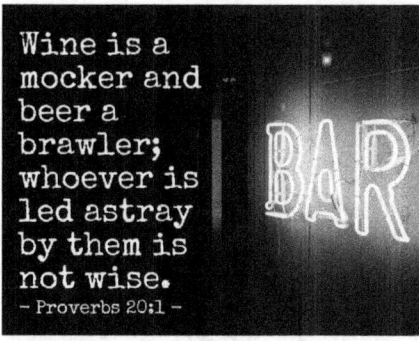

> Wine is a mocker and beer a brawler; whoever is led astray by them is not wise.
> – Proverbs 20:1 –

It wasn't long after this incident that I was in trouble with the law. I became rebellious to all authority, which brought on trouble and hardship to me, to those I knew, and to those I didn't know. Alcohol became my drug of choice. I loved the way it made me feel. It seemed to take away my problems and gave me a euphoric sense of courage; the courage I longed for and I saw in my older brother.

Looking back now, I realize alcohol was a false sense of security and brought nothing good in my life, only much destruction. I ended up in juvenile hall for a year. I was out of control. Instead of correcting my behavior, this experience hardened me and increased my rebellion towards authority. I rebelled from God, then my parents and school, and now the law.

I eventually quit school, got my GED, moved out of my parents' house and started working construction jobs. My drinking and partying lifestyle worsened. I went to jail many times for drunk-in-public and drunk driving charges. On my third driving under the influence (DUI) conviction, I was given a three year probation, a joint-suspended sentence, and was ordered to complete DUI classes. I completed the classes for the court, not for myself and continued drinking.

Over the years, when I was at a low point in my life and at my wits end, I always called on the name of Jesus. I now understand what a twinkling of an eye means, because that's how fast God came back into my life each time. Unfortunately, once He got me back on my feet and dusted me off, I went straight back to my drinking and destructive lifestyle.

I ended up breaking my probation and was sent to prison for three years. When I was released I violated my parole four times for alcohol-related events. I was given another three year prison sentence. Before I went to prison again on my second term, I asked Jesus to come back into my life. He did and for the next eight years, I simply lived closest to Him.

I got out of prison after eighteen months because of good time/work time credits. As I continued with the Lord, His blessings began to descend upon me. Prayers were being answered. I was married to the woman of my dreams. I had a great job. God was certainly blessing me. I had no need of anything. His peace in my heart was steadfast and perfect.

Toward the end of those eight years, I started feeling like I've really done well for myself. I was in control and things were good. One weekend I went golfing with some friends from work. Afterwards, they wanted to go to a brewery/restaurant. I didn't want to go but eventually relented to their request. I said to them that I wasn't going to drink, but I ended up drinking a few beers anyway.

I went backwards, as my drinking became worse than ever. My wife and I became separated, then divorced. The blessings God had given me now started to disappear one by one. God was inviting me and warning me to come back to Him. He used other people to talk to me to get me to stop drinking alcohol, but I would have none of it. I even made a mockery of their comments.

He gave me one last warning. I was having a poker game at my house and had about twenty minutes before my friends would arrive. I was alone, and the television was on a Christian channel. The person speaking said, "The Lord Jesus Christ says come back to Him today." I immediately felt the unseen force wanting to come back into my heart. I put out my hands and even turned my head to resist the Holy Spirit from coming back into my heart. I knew if I let God back into my heart, I could not continue my drunken, debaucherous lifestyle. This was a great mistake on my part!

One week later as I drove back home from the liquor store fear came over me. It was an aboding evil. I had never felt this sensation before. I was afraid to drive. I knew that I was going to be in a car wreck. One week later after drinking all night and into the next morning, my girlfriend said she had to leave for a bit and that she would be back. It was Easter morning, and I did not want her to leave.

A half hour after she left, I decided to go find her. I thought I knew where she went. I got in my truck and drove, but she was not there. On my way back home, I started to feel very intoxicated. I pulled over, called her on the phone and she asked, "Where are you?" She was already back at my house. I told her I didn't know and that I was really drunk. She wanted to pick me up and so did I, but I didn't know my location. I told her I would try to be there soon and hung up.

Right after that, I crashed my truck into a car full of people. A four year old boy died while most everyone else in the car was injured. Cops, and ambulances arrived. I was taken to the hospital, then to jail. When I was processed into the jail and was no longer drunk, I realized that my life was over and I was going to prison, probably for life. The full weight of what I had done, and my new future became very clear. I took the life of a child and injured others because of my choice to drive impaired. But, my pain is nothing compared to what I inflicted upon my victims.

I cried out to God once again. I called on the name of Jesus. Nothing happened as it had in times past. I began to plead and confess my sins, including the little boy's death and the injuries to the others, yet nothing happened. After an hour and a half, I became really scared. I thought I had crossed that invisible line of grace. It was a dreadful feeling that I had never experienced. I was not asking Jesus to get me out of this trouble, but to come back into my heart and be with me. I had to have the assurance of His presence in my heart. Bless God, my Lord and Savior Jesus Christ came back into my heart after one and half hours of praying.

I have been in prison eleven years of the fifteen year to life sentence and God is continually with me. I have been attending A.A. meetings for many years. It is a God-blessed program, and I see the spiritual principles in it. It is truly coming to God, repenting and then being discipled.

I hope and pray my story helps someone to make the right choice to not drive impaired as it leads to the road of destruction and misery.

IN HIS OWN WORDS
Hernan, Part-Time Uber Driver

My life is divided up between attending a university, starting my own business, working as a translator and driving for Uber on Friday and Saturday from eleven o'clock at night to four o'clock in the morning. This late night, early morning shift works for me because I am a night owl. Add to the fact that a premium fare is charged during this shift allows me to earn more money than daytime driving.

One can imagine the kind of people and things I experience when I drive this shift. But, the key is that when someone who has been drinking alcohol or partying all night calls Uber or any ride-share company, they are drinking responsibly. Whether college students, who are most likely underage to drink alcohol, or professionals, the fact that they recognize that their faculties are not functioning at the highest level is commendable.

The college students are usually party hopping from one fraternity house to another, whereas the professionals usually use Uber after celebrating a special event. When an impaired customer enters my car, I always tell them that they made a wise decision to use ride-share, and then proceed to drive them to their final destination. Most of the riders know better and many of them have stories to share with me. It is amazing how alcohol will loosen people up, which leads them to share their life stories with me; subsequently the person typically asks for my advice. In fact, one man shared that he was having marital problems and asked me for marriage advice. Chuckling to myself, I explained to him that I was single and suggested he talk to his wife about his concerns.

Some of the riders have shared that they have had a previous DUI(s) and under no circumstances do they ever want to have to deal with all the events that are associated with impaired driving. Some have shared that they no longer drink alcohol and drive because they refuse to pay the one thousand dollars required to install a breathalyzer on their car. They decided it was better to use Uber, than drive and take the chance of being arrested for DUI, again.

There are also those social drinkers who were out for a good time and needed a ride home. I had been driving only a short time when I received a request to drive two intoxicated women to their respective destinations. That ride impacted me because the two women were medical doctors. They were so drunk that one barfed on the backseat floor. The other lifted her shirt and barfed into it, which was courteous. The car reeked of vomit and I was mad! Now, I had to clean up someone's mess due to excessive alcohol consumption. At least, the doctor threw up into her blouse and apologized. Not wanting to clean up the mess, I paid my neighbor twenty dollars to clean my car. I was back in business the next night.

Being a single man, it is surprising how women become loose when they are drunk. I have been propositioned, invited to parties and have been asked to sing along with groups of girls who are having a night on the town. I always allow my riders to play their music as I drive them to their desired location. Often the young ladies will offer me an extra tip if I will sing with them. We have the Uber version of *Carpool Karaoke* taking place as I drive the girls. It's fun and makes the drive entertaining. Singing with and driving drunk young ladies for an extra tip is always an experience.

Speaking of tips, those who use my ride service due to being intoxicated often offer me tips above and beyond what is entered into the Uber *app* as they exit my car. Often, I am asked if I smoke or if they could tip me with marijuana. I always reply no, but sometimes I have found a joint in the backseat at the end of the night. One time, I picked up a woman who owned a successful pastry shop in town. She tipped me with some wonderful tasting pastries. Again, I didn't need the pastries, but they sure were *delicioso!*

It amazes me how someone who has been partying all

night is willing to share their life story to a complete, but trusted stranger. I write trusted, as the rider is trusting me to drive them to their destination without incident. Many times, the rider asks me if I have been drinking as they enter the car. They assume that because they are inebriated that I am too. I assure the person I am not intoxicated with a definitive NO! Besides the rider trusting me with a safe ride home, they end up talking candidly.

One rider hopped into my car *drunk as a skunk* and began telling me how he was well-known in his profession to the point of being egotistical. Since I didn't believe what he was telling me, I called his bluff and asked him a very pointed question. He knew the answer. Just to be sure he wasn't *handing me a line,* after working that evening and early morning I went home and searched his name on the internet. Sure enough, he was who he said he was. One thing I have learned since becoming an Uber driver, all kinds of people drink alcohol for all kinds of reasons.

The point I want to *drive home* is that if you drink alcohol, don't drive. Drinking responsibly means drinking with wisdom. Wisdom is having a sober designated driver take you around town if you want to drink enough alcohol that would increase your legal blood alcohol concentration (BAC) level above 0.08. Wisdom is calling a ride-share company such as Uber. Wisdom is recognizing that if you started your evening driving your car, but become buzzed, leave the car behind and take another form of transportation. Wisdom is calling a family member or friend and asking for a ride home instead of driving yourself. Wisdom is keeping yourself and other people who are on the road unharmed by recognizing that you are not capable of driving.

I meet a lot of interesting people in the wee hours of the morning. Each one with their own reason for using Uber, but all of them have one thing in common, they have the wherewithal to know that they are not capable of driving home safely. There are many options for getting home safely, please do not drive impaired.

ABOUT THE RESPONSIBLY DRIVEN DUI PROJECT

In 2014, a group of DUI murderers, at the California Training Facility (CTF) – Soledad, came together to discuss their shared experiences. As a group, we committed ourselves to discovering the underlying issues that led to our substance abuse and driving under the influence (DUI). As these meetings progressed, we found that using a more specific approach to DUI prevention produced greater insight into our choice to drive impaired. Seeing the progress we made, our goals shifted. We wanted to offer our newly acquired tools and insights to other DUI offenders, so we created *Responsibly Driven*.

Responsibly Driven is a program developed by DUI offenders to affect long-term change in those arrested for, or who are at risk of driving under the influence. Our curriculum meets DUI offenders at their level of responsibility, while challenging their destructive beliefs and behaviors.

Our approach to DUI prevention is what makes *Responsibly Driven* unique. The curriculum treats DUI as a series of choices; we make a choice to become intoxicated, and then we make an additional choice to drive under the influence. The purpose of *Responsibly Driven* is to help participants better understand both of these choices.

Our program further assists participants to identify and address their underlying issues with DUI through our *CS3 Sobriety Plan*. *Responsibly Driven* participants leave our program with a **C**lean, **S**ober, **S**afe and **S**ustainable plan for sobriety and DUI prevention. *Responsibly Driven* currently facilitates its curriculum in small group sessions at two California state prisons.

As members of *Responsibly Driven,* we seek to raise awareness of the destructive force this preventable tragedy inflicts upon victims, their families and the community.

LETTER FROM THE PUBLISHER

Let the lamentations of the prisoner come before You; according to the greatness of Your power preserve those who are sentenced to life in prison.

Psalm 79:11 (Paraphrased)

IMPACT: Insights, Effects and the Reality of Impaired Driving is a book of lamentations from inmates who have committed DUI murder. There is no excuse for impaired driving – it is a one hundred-percent preventable crime. The inmates share their stories in hopes that others learn from their arrogance, denial and personal experiences. Others affected by impaired driving share their perspective and the effect it had on their life.

Many of the inmates are sentenced to prison for life; but their voices can still be *heard* through this book. I read the inmates testimonials to understand why people drive under the influence. My eyes were opened to the reasons and excuses people use to justify drinking and driving. I learned that the intent of the book is to prevent others from impaired driving. It was a new perspective for prevention – learn from other's mistakes.

Chris Martinez and the men's willingness to share their stories started as a grassroots movement to help stop the pervasive problem of impaired driving. Yet, it goes beyond drinking – drugs, texting and distracted driving also cause auto collisions and the loss of life.

The original publisher of the book, Amends Publishing, sent me a copy of the letter that they originally mailed to the contributing inmates. It included the following paragraphs:

Early this year, Amends Publishing experienced a fire from which we will be unable to recover; thus, Amends Publishing is closing its doors. The good news is the DUI book, which was so very close to completion and publication, is not going to be abandoned. Fortunately, Fiesta Publishing is enthusiastic about pursuing the project.

Something notable: Everything on the premises was either scorched, melted, or incinerated; however, your personally handwritten or typed stories that were stored in a dedicated reinforced cardboard filing cabinet – did not burn! We consider that miraculous! God's special protection of your stories.

When I read that the cardboard box, which contained all the handwritten and typed stories, had survived the fire, I ascertained that the various perspectives of DUI murder needed to be shared with others. As the publisher of *IMPACT*, I, in conjunction with the inmates and the writers of other perspectives, hope to bring a greater awareness to the systemic problem of impaired driving and to start a dialogue for successful prevention measures.

Fiesta Publishing believes that by publishing this book, change will come.

Julie Castro
Fiesta Publishing

ACKNOWLEDGEMENTS

The publication of this book is the result of untiring effort and continual support from several persons:

Thank you to all the authors – Allison Jacobszoon, Brian Hamlin, Cari Fonseca, Charles Callion, Chris Martinez, Chris Reinoso, Conrado Rivera, Daniel Ruiz, Darrell, David Lewis, David Thorne, Deborah White, DeVyon Walker, Douglas Doyle, Eduardo Alvarez, Edward Collins, Eric Dungan, Gerardo Palacios, Heather Azkoul, Hernan Castro, Jennifer Swenson, Jim Crawford, Jonathan P.M. Barber, Jonathan Garcia, Juan Covarrubias, Kellie Byers, the Law Enforcement Officer, Leroy Stotts, Maria Lopez, Mark Saunders, Michael Baldwin, Sr., Nancy, Paul Belmontez, Peter Barragan, Peter Weiland, Rae Ellen Foy, Raymond Moura, Rudy Lopez, Sergio Dávalos, and Stephen Watson – for your generous, candid and poignant testimonials. They are the heartbeat of this book.

A special thanks to Jim Crawford and Gerardo Palacios for being the first courageous contributors to this project of healing.

Thank you to the Covarrubias family – Juan Covarrubias, Etlinn Delgado, Victorina Gomez, Horacio Covarrubias, Paola Covarrubias, Rick Rodriguez, and Oscar Espino – for your generous donation. A special thanks to Juan, our Marketing Coordinator, for your fervid patronage, which made this project possible. We are grateful for all the hard work you gave to this effort.

Thank you to Eusebio S. Martinez for your financial contribution and love. To Sharon Bignall and Petra Martinez Ali for your unconditional love.

Thank you to AMB for your hardened commitment to restorative justice through the establishment of Amends Publishing as our first platform to share our testimonials. Also, thank you to D. and S. Po. for helping convicted criminals make amends through this endeavor.

Thank you to Edward Collins for your enthusiastic advocacy and continuous encouragement throughout this entire project.

Thank you to Julie Castro for your valuable expertise and advice. Your diligence and enthusiasm throughout this publishing process has been absolutely priceless.

Thank you to Pastor Jordan Jeske, Cornerstone New Hope Ministry, and The Urban Ministry Institute (TUMI) instructors – Mari Ole, Pastor John Boic and Pastor Scott Stroud – for your inspiration, guidance, and mentorship.

Thank you to the other founding members of *Responsibly Driven* – Jason Dalby, Eric Dungan, Michael Ingram, Kevin McGuiness, Victor Mendibles, Luis Parada, Christopher Wachniuk, and Bruce Walker – for your insightful life coaching and friendship. A special thanks to Christopher for initiating the formation of *Responsibly Driven,* Eric for assisting in the development of *Responsibly Driven's* **C**lean, **S**ober, **S**afe and **S**ustainable *(CS3)* curriculum, and Bruce for critiquing many of the book's sections.

Thank you to all the people who protect society from impaired drivers and heal the wounds of those most affected by impaired driving.

APPENDICES

ACRONYMS AND TERMS

Administrative Segregation Unit (ASU) - Solitary confinement for violent or disruptive behavior. Inmates are typically housed in a single prison cell twenty-three hours a day and allowed only one hour outside the cell for exercise and a shower.

Alcoholics Anonymous (A.A.) - A Twelve-Step recovery program that focuses on alcoholism.

Al-Anon - A support group for individuals who have friends and/or family members struggling with alcoholism.

App - An application, typically a small, specialized program downloaded onto mobile devices.

Bender - A slang term for a series of days, even weeks of heavy intoxication.

Blackout - A state of unconsciousness caused by intoxication. A person in a blackout is functional, but his/her memory retention is faulty. Typically, she/he will not recall the previous day's behavior.

Blood Alcohol Concentration (BAC) Level - Alcohol related DUIs are determined by a person's BAC level. In the US, alcohol-impaired driving is defined as a driver with a BAC level of 0.08 or higher.

Board of Prison Hearings (BHP: also known as the *Board*) - BHPs conduct parole suitability hearings in order to determine if an inmate with an indeterminate (life) sentence is suitable to be released from prison.

Carpool Karaoke - A recurring segment on *The Late Late Show with James Corden,* in which James invites famous musical guests to sing along to their songs as he drives. This term is used to describe Uber passengers singing to music of their choice, as the driver takes the customer to their destination.

CO - An acronym for Correctional Officers. COs are the custody staff that provide supervision and security in prisons.

Coded - A slang term used to describe a patient whose heart has stopped beating, as in cardiac arrest.

Cop Shop - A slang term for a police station.

CS3 - An acronym used by the *Responsibly Driven* curriculum to describe the sobriety and its DUI prevention plan: **C**lean, **S**ober, **S**afe and **S**ustainable.

Drafts of Fuel - A slang term for alcohol.

Driving Under the Influence (DUI) - A legal term that refers to the criminal act of impaired driving. Some states use the following terms:
- Driving While Intoxicated (DWI)
- Operating Under the Influence (OUI)

Drunkfest - A slang term that describes binge drinking which includes five or more alcoholic beverages in one sitting.

Field Sobriety Test (FST) - A battery of tests used by law enforcement officers to determine if a person suspected of impaired driving is intoxicated with drugs or alcohol.

Give a Rip - An euphemism for a profane expression, describing a wanton and callous disregard.

Great Bodily Injury (GBI) - A legal term that describes the severity of an individual's injury. Such a designation is an aggravating factor which will enhance an offender's criminal charges and punishment.

Gross Vehicular Manslaughter (GVM) - The unlawful killing of a human being with gross negligence, typically while driving a vehicle under the influence (of alcohol).

High - A slang term that describes a state of drug intoxication.

Highlife - A slang term that describes a lifestyle of a drug addict and/or alcoholic.

Hot-box - A slang term that describes the practice of smoking marijuana in a car with the windows closed. The goal is to fill up the car with as much smoke as possible.

Kegger - A slang term for a party at which beer is served, typically from kegs.

Macho - A term that describes a toxic paradigm of masculinity.

Maintenance Drinker - Drinking alcohol at a rate intended to maintain the current level of intoxication. (Urbandictionary.com).

Mud - A slang term for alcohol.

Narcotics Anonymous (NA) - A Twelve-Step program that focuses on drug addiction.

Party Hard - A slang saying describing an outing full of heavy binge drinking and/or drug usage.

Pruno - A slang term for prison wine made from apples, oranges, fruit cocktail, candy, ketchup, sugar, and possibly other ingredients. Bread is included for its yeast to stimulate fermentation.

Preliminary Alcohol Screening (PAS) - A test used by law enforcement to measure your BAC level. The PAS device is a hand-held breath-testing unit that gives an instant and accurate measure of your BAC level.

Rate - An abbreviated term that refers to insurance rates. Insurance companies use different rating criteria, such as age, number of miles driven over a year, driving history, and a resident's location, to determine the premium for the auto owner.

Rules Violation Report (RVR) - Inmates who violate written or posted rules are subject to disciplinary sanctions. When an inmate commits an act contrary to the rules, a reporting form called a Rule Violation Report (RVR) will be filed.
Second Degree Murder – Any intentional murder with malice aforethought, but is not premeditated or planned. The conviction tends to carry an indeterminate sentence (life term).

SR-22 and FR-44 Insurance Form - The SR-22 and FR-44 are certificates of financial responsibility that many states require when you apply to get your driver's license reinstated after a DUI. These certificates are not limited to just alcohol-related driving offenses. They are also related to DWIs and OUIs. Your insurance company must file these certificates with the DMV on your behalf.

Team Brandon - *The Next Step Foundation Team Brandon* is a non-profit organization based in Arizona. Team Brandon presents it's story from the offender's point of view about the life-altering effects of drinking and driving to schools and community groups throughout Phoenix. Team Brandon holds their annual *Vow to Drive Sober 5K/1 Mile Educational Event and Expo* in December. (http://TeamBrandon.org).

Torn Up - A slang saying that describes a state of high intoxication.

Wasted - A slang term that describes a state of high intoxication.

DISCUSSION QUESTIONS

Use following questions to initiate either a small group discussion or a candid conversation with a loved one about impaired driving and substance abuse.

Discussion Questions about DUI Offenders' Testimonials:

1. What aspect(s) of the testimonials do you most identify with, and why?

2. How did alcohol and/or drugs affect the author's life? How do alcohol and/or drugs affect your life?

3. What did the author believe he/she could not do sober, and why? What do you believe you cannot do sober, and why?

4. How did peer pressure affect the author's decision to drink alcohol and/or use drugs? And to drive impaired? How does peer pressure affect your decision to drink alcohol and/or use drugs? And to drive impaired?

5. What reasons did the author give for not heeding warning signs (e.g., Internal Warning Signs: negative thoughts and uncomfortable feelings; External Warning Signs: DUI arrests, auto collisions, injuries, court fines, admonishments from friends and family, etc.)? What warning signs have you ignored?

6. What excuses did the author used to justify his/her decision to drive impaired? What excuses have you used to drive impaired?

7. What specific consequences did the author describe? What are the consequences of your substance abuse? And impaired driving?

8. What people did the author identify as being impacted by his/her impaired driving? How many victims can you identify? What people are being impacted by your substance abuse? And impaired driving?

9. What did the author do to address his/her substance abuse? And impaired driving? What else could he/she have done? What do you plan to do address your substance abuse? And impaired driving?

10. How did the author express his/her accountability? How was the author unaccountable for his/her decision(s)? How can you express your accountability for your irresponsible choice(s)?

11. How did the author express his/her remorse? What could he/she done more of to show his/her remorse?

12. Finish the following statements:
   a. "The first time I drove impaired was ..."
   b. "Since that time, I have driven impaired X times ..."
   c. "If I do not stop driving impaired, I will totally ..."
   d. "If I stop driving impaired, I might be able to ..."
   e. "I now recognize ..."

Discussion Questions About the Other DUI Testimonials:

1. What aspects of the testimonial do you most identify with, and why?

2. Describe the author's experience of impaired driving. What thoughts and feelings did the author describe about the general experience of impaired driving? And the impaired driver?

3. How was the author's life altered by impaired driving?

4. What physical injuries did the author sustain?

5. What was the financial impact?

6. What emotional and mental trauma did the author describe?

7. How was the author's family life affected? Social life? Professional life?

8. What did the author want to happen with the impaired driver, and why?

9. What types of amends does the impaired driver owe to the author?

10. What solutions did the author offer to prevent their occurrence of impaired driving?

General Discussion Questions:

1. After reading the testimonials from various perspectives, what new insight did you gain about substance abuse and impaired driving?

2. What assumptions do people make about impaired drivers?

3. What assumptions does the criminal justice system make in response to impaired driving and substance abuse?

4. What assumptions do people make about the victims and survivors of impaired driving?

5. What is necessary to examine these assumptions in an honest, compassionate, and responsible manner?

6. Why have existing solutions to impaired driving worked? Why have existing solutions not worked? What are somenew possible solutions?

7. What needs to happen to bring all sides together to make impaired driving *a thing of the past?*

www.ingramcontent.com/pod-product-compliance
Lightning Source LLC
Chambersburg PA
CBHW070552010526
44118CB00012B/1296